ENCYCLOPEDIA OF

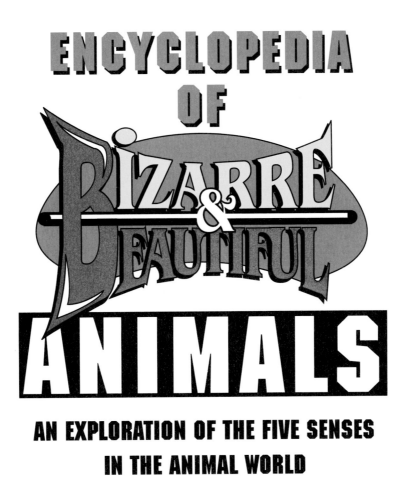

ANIMALS

AN EXPLORATION OF THE FIVE SENSES
IN THE ANIMAL WORLD

Santa Fe Writers Group

John Muir Publications
Santa Fe, New Mexico

Special thanks to Dr. Mary Colleen McNamara, Department of Biology,
Albuquerque Technical-Vocational Institute and Dr. Marvin Riedesel,
Department of Biology, University of New Mexico.

Santa Fe Writers Group:
Miriam Bobkoff, research
Donald E. Fineberg
A. S. Gintzler
Miriam Sagan
Leda Silver

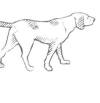

John Muir Publications
P.O. Box 613, Santa Fe, New Mexico 87504

Printed in the United States of America
First edition. First printing January 1998.

Material in this edition previously published by John Muir Publications in the
Bizarre & Beautiful series.

Logo/Interior Design: Ken Wilson
Illustrations: Chris Brigman
Printer: Worzalla, Stevens Point, Wisconsin

ISBN: 1-56261-416-9

Cover photo: Common Iguana, Animals Animals © E.R. Degginger

CONTENTS

GOOD VIBRATIONS

Sound is made of **vibrations** produced by movement. The movement can be as slight as a ladybug crawling on a blade of grass or as large as a hurricane ripping through a town. These vibrations travel in **waves**. Though light can travel through a vacuum like outer space, sound cannot. It needs a medium to travel through. Usually that medium is air, water, or earth.

Sound waves are vibrations produced by movement, no matter how small.

The average human speaking voice measures around 60 decibels. A rock band plays at over 120 decibels. Sounds above 140 decibels, such as jet planes taking off, can be painful to your ears, and possibly even injure them.

Our sense of hearing helps us communicate with each other and avoid danger. It is also our key to the world of beautiful sounds.

Sounds can have different pitches; they can be high or low or somewhere in between. Pitch is determined by the **frequency** of the sound waves—the number of vibrations they produce in a second. A high-frequency sound, such as fingernails scraping a blackboard, has a high pitch. A low-frequency sound—thunder, for example—has a low pitch. Frequency is measured in **hertz**. The normal range for humans is 20 to 20,000 hertz. Bats, cats, dogs, and other animals can hear sounds of far higher frequency, called **ultrasound**. In fact, bats produce and hear high-pitched ultrasound that measures over 100,000 hertz! Sounds also vary in volume—how loud or soft they are. This is called **intensity** and is measured in **decibels**.

AN AUDITORY ASSORTMENT

Not all ears are alike—far from it. Mammals' ears are on the sides or the tops of their heads. But crickets' ears are on their legs, and moths' ears are under their wings! Some ears are very simple while others, like our own, are complex organs.

Some ears are big and floppy, others are small and pointy. But if they're made of skin, you know they belong to a mammal. Land mammals are the only animals with fleshy outer ears, called **pinnae**. You've probably seen rabbits prick up their tall ears when

BALANCING ACT

Have you ever spun yourself around and around until you collapsed dizzily to the floor? What you did was upset your **balance**. To be exact, you sent scrambled messages to your brain, so it was unable to make the necessary adjustments that keep you upright.

Structures in the inner ear gather balance-sensing information and send it to the brain. This is why an injury to your ear can sometimes make you feel "woozy" or unsteady on your feet. Some organs in your ear work to maintain balance while you are still—sitting down, for example. These are called the **saccule** and **utricle**. The **semicircular canals** tell your brain when you are about to lose your balance during movement. If you're about to fall off your bicycle, for example, this organ will alert your brain so it can tell the right muscles to save you from toppling over.

Your eyes and special cells in the soles of your feet and the joints of your arms and legs also help keep you right-side-up.

In many animals, ears serve not only to hear but to help maintain balance.

they're listening, and lay them down flat when they're munching on grass. Humans cannot move their pinnae like this to channel sound into the ear, but some people *can* contract their ear muscles—otherwise known as "wiggling" their ears.

Birds and most reptiles and marine mammals have ear slits on the sides of their head. This ear slit is called the **auditory canal**. Fish do not have any outer ears at all, not even ear slits. They pick up sound vibrations through their skin and pass it on to their inner ears.

The Path of Sound

Despite all of these different kinds of ears, there are some common elements to the sense of hearing. First, sound waves enter the ear and hit the **eardrum**, or **tympanic membrane**. (Animals with no outer ears sense sound waves through bone or tissue.) The eardrum passes the sound waves to the **middle** and **inner ear**, where they are changed into electrical nerve signals that are sent to the brain. The brain then perceives (understands) these signals as sound.

This book can only give you a glimpse of all the fascinating things there are to learn about ears and hearing. But it will introduce you to many of the interesting ways animals relate to their environment and to each other. We hope this book sparks you to learn more about the sense of hearing. If you want to review a term (*sound wave*, for example), or if you come across a word you don't understand (what's *ultrasound*?), turn to the glossarized index at the back. But first, let's enter the bizarre and beautiful world of ears.

Moths

(Order: Lepidoptera)

We don't usually expect ears to grow out of the chest, but that's where moths' ears are: just below the second pair of wings. The moth has the simplest known auditory (hearing) system in the animal kingdom. Its primitive "ears" are made up of a tympanic membrane (its "eardrum") and two acoustic sensory cells. One of these cells is more sensitive than the other. Together they are tuned to pick up ultrasound and are especially alert to the calls of bats. Why bats? Because these flying mammals are the moth's main predator. Humans cannot hear the high-pitched sounds that bats make when they chirp, but moths can. They can even tell how far away a bat is.

Imagine if you had two wings flapping up and down over your ears. It might make it difficult to hear. The same goes for moths. They hear much better when their wings are on the upstroke, exposing the tympanic membrane. With its two "ears," the moth can listen in different directions. And it can hear both loud and soft sounds. If a bat's cries are faint and far away, the moth will turn and fly in the opposite direction. But if the bat is gaining fast, the moth will respond with escape tactics. The fleeing moth might make loops in the air, or fold its wings and drop suddenly to the ground. The result is an aerial battle in which the moth still has a chance for survival.

MUSICAL MOTHS

People used to think that moths were tone-deaf, but a summer dinner party suggested otherwise. When a guest ran his wet finger around the rim of a glass, making a ringing sound, dozens of moths dropped to the ground from where they had been fluttering around paper lanterns. The professor who was giving the party was intrigued and began to research moths. Scientists soon discovered that moths react to many musical sounds.

To escape a bat, some moths make loops in the air. Others fold their wings and drop to the ground.

8

Pericopid moth, above and facing page

Crickets

(Family: Gryllidae)

Moths have ears beneath their wings. Mosquitoes listen with antennae on top of their head, and crickets' ears are on their front legs. Their hearing is directional, which means they have to point their ears at the sound itself. Imagine listening to a conversation by pointing your knees towards the speaker!

The cricket's ears, like the ears of other insects, are very simple, just an eardrum and nerves that pick up sound vibration. It is a basic system, yet many insects can hear beyond the normal range for human ears.

In the cricket world, only the males sing. Crickets produce their song by rubbing parts of their body together. The short-horned field cricket, for example, moves its back legs up and down. On the inside of each leg, there is a row of tiny teeth that scrapes against the forewing, creating the song. Some crickets sing by rubbing their forewings together.

Male crickets sing one song to attract the female cricket into the area, and a different one to court her once she's there. Sometimes a group of males sing together in a loud chorus, drawing several females to them. Interestingly, the song of one cricket species won't attract a female from another species. Two species of insects simply don't understand each other—it's as if one were speaking Spanish and the other Russian! Crickets also sing to drive away other males. This is especially true of the type of cricket who lives alone in a burrow and sings to defend its territory.

Nisitrus cricket

SONG OF LIFE

The field grasshopper, a cousin of the cricket, has a song for *every* important occasion—and if you're a grasshopper, there are only three. The "calling song" is a long melody designed to attract the female. If two males meet, they burst into the "rival's song." This short tune has strong aggressive accents. If a female joins them, they begin chirping the "courting song."

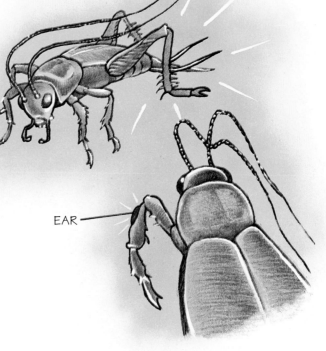

EAR

The cricket's simple ears are on its front legs.

Saddle-backed bush cricket, facing page

Drum Fish

(Equetus punctatus)

How did the drum fish get its name? From its peculiar grunting, which sounds like a drumbeat. The drum fish has no vocal organs like mammals and birds. It produces its "drumbeat" by rapidly contracting and expanding muscles to vibrate its air bladder. (This motion can be as fast as 24 times per second!) The air bladder is a gas-filled sac in the abdominal (belly) cavity, between the fish's spine and intestines. It helps keep the fish at the ocean depth it prefers. When the walls of the air bladder vibrate, the sound resonates and is projected out into the water.

Drum fishes, like all fishes, lack an outer ear. So how do they hear each other? They pick up sound vibrations through the sides of their bodies and collect them with their air bladders. The air bladder then passes the sound vibrations on to four small structures (called the Weberian apparatus) in the fish's middle ear. From there, the vibrations travel to the fish's inner ear, or labyrinth. (It's called a labyrinth because it resembles a maze.) Next, the fluids in the labyrinth jiggle. Tiny hair cells in the labyrinth pick up the jiggle and flash signals to the fish's brain.

The middle and inner ears of people and fish are alike in many ways. The air bladder of the fish's middle ear is similar to the eardrum in mammals. The fish's Weberian apparatus is similar to four tiny bones in your own ear. The fluids in the inner ears of fish and humans are pretty much the same, too.

A FISHY SOUND

Are fish quiet? Not at all. The reason we do not hear their acoustic signals is that most fish noises are reflected back from the surface and stay underwater. But advances in the science of underwater bioacoustics (the sounds made by living things) reveal a wide variety of sounds produced by fish. Did you know that, in general, ocean fish hear mainly low notes, and freshwater fish hear mainly high notes?

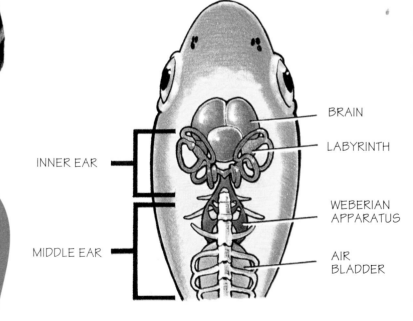

Many fishes, including the drum fish, collect sound vibrations with their air bladder.

Spotted drum fish, above and facing page

FROGS

When it comes to croaking, frogs are the experts. Frog calls consist of both low- and high-frequency vibrations that resonate like human vowel sounds. Frogs make many kinds of calls: mating calls, warning and distress calls, calls of territory ownership, and calls in response to other calls. Often, these have harmonic structures that remind us of music. Have you ever heard a frog chorus in full swing? Step on a twig or make some slight noise and they'll all fall silent. Frogs' sensitive ears alert them to potential danger.

Frogs have no outer ear like we do to capture and direct sound to the inner ear. If you look closely behind a frog's eyes, you'll see two round disks. These are the frog's tympanic membranes, the animal's eardrums. When sounds hit the tightly stretched membrane, it jiggles and passes the vibrations along a small bone to the inner ear labyrinth. This labyrinth is a system of sacs and canals that passes vibrations on to the auditory nerves. In turn, these nerves pass impulses to the frog's brain, which understands the impulses as sound.

Frogs need their ears for more than hearing. The inner ear labyrinth maintains a frog's equilibrium, or balance. If the labyrinth is damaged, a frog loses its ability to sit upright, to swim, or to coordinate its leg movements. Without their ears, frogs would dive, dip, and dunk dizzily.

European tree frog

FROM LUNG TO DRUM

Frogs start out as fish-like tadpoles that live in water. In a process called metamorphosis, they grow legs, absorb their tails, and undergo other changes to become amphibious frogs. Amphibians are animals that are able to live both in and out of water. Tadpoles' ears change, too. Frogs have eardrums to hear on dry land, but tadpoles don't. Instead, tadpoles pick up vibrations with their lungs.

Tadpoles don't develop ears until they're adult frogs. Until then, they "hear" with their lungs.

Giant tree frog, facing page

SNAKES

(Order: Squamata)

A snake charmer plays his flute as a cobra rises from its basket, swaying to the music—or so it seems. Is the snake really "charmed" by the music? Can the snake even hear the haunting melody it seems to dance to?

The answer is no. Snakes have neither outer ears nor middle ear cavities. But they aren't deaf. Their hearing is quite good for detecting low-frequency sounds carried through ground vibrations. Thudding footsteps, for instance, vibrate through the ground and are picked up by a snake's jaw bones, then carried through other bones to the inner ear. The inner ear is a system of tubes which are filled with a fluid. The fluid passes vibrations to a duct called a cochlea. It is shaped like a snail's shell and named after the Greek word for snail. There, tiny hair cells pick up the vibrations, turn them into a signal the brain can understand, then send them to the brain which interprets the vibrations as sound.

Rough green snake

A researcher named Colonel Wells tested cobras' response to noise. He blindfolded the snakes, then walked nearby, causing the ground to vibrate. The snakes reared up, spread their hoods, and faced the direction of his footsteps. When he stood still and blew a bugle, the snakes didn't react at all! But some snakes *do* react to some airborne sounds. Does this mean that cobras can hear the music of snake charmers after all?

No. "Charmed" cobras are actually responding to the moving arms and legs of their charmers—which they see with their eyes.

SNAKES ON LAND

Snakes and other reptiles were the first vertebrates (animals with backbones) to lay their eggs on land. They were an important part of animals' evolution from water to land. In the inner ear of snakes and other reptiles are similarities to the ears of humans and other mammals.

Snakes "hear" ground vibrations, such as footsteps and the movement of prey, through their jaw bones.

Yellow rat snake, facing page

16

Kangaroo Rats

(Genera *Dipodomys* and *Microdipodops*)

The kangaroo rat is a small nocturnal rodent that lives in desert areas. Both the rattlesnake and the owl like to dine on the kangaroo rat. The rattlesnake has the unique ability to sense the heat given off by warm-blooded prey such as the kangaroo rat. And the owl has keen vision and spectacular hearing, more precise than radar itself. How can the kangaroo rat possibly escape from these powerful predators?

By using its extra-sensitive hearing, that's how. The rodent's ears not only hear but actually amplify (make louder) sounds such as that of an owl's beating wings. Kangaroo rats can even detect the sound of an owl gliding, its wings outspread. (Humans can hear this soundless flight only when it is amplified electronically.)

Just as the owl is about to snatch up the kangaroo rat in its sharp talons, the rodent leaps into the air like the kangaroo it is named after. It can jump at least a foot away from where the owl strikes, empty-clawed.

Just before it strikes, a rattlesnake makes a sound—often too faint for humans to hear. The sound may be a rattle or a hiss or just the glide of scales along the ground. But the kangaroo rat hears the snake clearly, and once again makes a leap to safety.

Chisel-toothed kangaroo rat

MIDDLE EAR FOR LOW RANGE

The ear of the kangaroo rat is unusual. Its middle ear cavity is much bigger than in other animals its size. Its large middle ear enables the kangaroo rat to hear low-frequency sound waves. And that is just the range it needs to detect the rattlesnake's slither or the owl's whoosh of wings.

The kangaroo rat leaps to safety thanks to its ability to hear the faint sound a rattlesnake makes before it strikes.

Desert kangaroo rat, facing page

Foxes

(Genus: *Vulpes*)

You would hear nothing, but fox ears are so sensitive they can hear the high-pitched squeak of insect larvae in the ground. The bat-eared fox of southwest Africa claws the ground at night, hunting for termites and dung beetle larvae. Sound tasty? To the bat-eared fox, there is nothing tastier. Insects are the main ingredient of its diet.

Foxes have a keen sense of hearing, which they use for listening to each other, as well as to insects. Pups listen for their parents' call. When they hear the high whistling sound of the adult foxes, the pups leave their snug underground burrow to join their parents. When foxes groom each other, they make a satisfied peeping sound. When bat-eared foxes "argue" over food, they growl at each other, sounding a lot like small dogs. When a fox is cornered or captured by predators or human hunters, it yelps and woofs.

The way a fox holds its ears reflects what it is doing and how it feels. For example, a fox points its ears forward when it is alert and listening. When startled or distressed, the ears lie down flat against the head, similar to a hissing cat. (By the way, foxes are related to dogs and wolves, not cats, as many people think.) And if a fox is threatened, it lays its ears down and turns the black insides of the ears forward, trying to look fierce.

Cape fox

HOT AND COLD EARS

The fennec fox of north Africa and the bat-eared fox of southwest Africa have tall, dramatic ears. These ears have a large surface area with many blood vessels that disperse heat. This helps the foxes endure the scorching temperature of their desert habitat (living space). The arctic fox lives in an extremely cold region. It has to keep its body heat inside. To survive the freezing temperatures, the fox exposes less surface area. What size ears do you suppose the arctic fox has? You guessed it: very small ones.

Once the fox hears the high-pitched squeak of insect larvae, it claws the ground in search of a snack.

Fennec fox, facing page

Bats

(Order: Chiroptera)

Bennett's spear-nosed bat

Blind as a bat? Actually, bats see better than people do—but they "see" with their ears! A bat can zero in on a moth and snatch it out of thin air at 60 miles an hour on a pitch black night, blindfolded. Wow! How? Bats form complex mental pictures of their surroundings by emitting short bursts of sound that bounce off objects and back to their ears. These bouncing sounds are known as echoes, and this method of "seeing" is called echolocation. There are more than 900 species of bats worldwide, but it is the insect-eating bats who are the champs of echolocation. (Their eyes are so weak that they can barely tell whether it's day or night.)

It all starts in the bat's throat, where the animal produces high-frequency sounds that shoot out through its mouth or nose, sometimes both. The bat's outer ears (pinnae) are very flexible and highly sensitive. They listen carefully to the echoes of their squeaks and can tell how far away an object is by how long it takes for the echo to return. Bats can detect insects up to 18 feet (about 5.5 meters) away. Bats' super-sensitive ears also can determine the shape of an insect or other object by the way the sound has changed when it comes back as an echo.

Although bats make many noises that humans can hear, we can't detect the ultrasonic beeps they use for echolocation. Ultrasound is very high-frequency sound, way beyond the range humans can hear. (*Ultra* means high.) So, when you see a bat swooping after moths on a summer night, you can be sure they're beeping and squeaking like mad—even though you can't hear a thing.

ANTENNAE EARS

A lively pair of ears is essential in echo-location. Bats can move their pinnae (outer ears) very rapidly—as fast as six times per second—while using them as echo receivers. Horseshoe bats can move each ear in different directions, but most bats move both ears in the same direction.

Bats use echolocation to hunt moths, one of their favorite foods.

Long-eared bat, facing page

SHRews

(Genus: *Sorex*)

These small mammals live in underground tunnel systems, often along rivers or wet meadows. Their ears vary somewhat depending on their habitat. For example, those in cooler climates have hairy ears for warmth, while those in tropical areas have naked ears.

Shrews are a "talkative" bunch. They use a variety of sounds to communicate with each other. If a baby shrew falls out of its tunnel nest or is hungry, it will bark until its mother appears. Mothers and infants also whisper to each other, which may serve as their way of recognizing each other.

Some shrews shriek when they are startled, probably to scare off predators. Shrews "talk" three different ways: they hiss through their nose, click with their tongue, and vocalize from their larynx, the vocal organ in the throat. (To vocalize means to make sound with vocal organs, in contrast to making sound by, say, clapping your hands.)

The shrew's high-pitched twitter serves a special purpose. Some of these sounds are actually ultrasonic (very high-frequency) and work by echolocation to help the shrew find its way around, especially in the dim light or darkness of its tunnel world. The shrew bounces its own voice off surrounding obstacles and, through the returning "echo," gets a clearer picture of its environment.

Shrews also use hearing to hunt. When a shrew hears a rustling noise, it immediately leaps to investigate. Shrews sniff about in their burrows or through the undergrowth until they find the insect larvae they like to munch on. But while they may be bold with small critters like insect larvae, shrews are generally very cautious. Before leaving its burrow, the shrew sticks out its snout. It is smelling for danger but also clicking and whistling, using echolocation to determine whether it's safe to come out.

Elephant shrew

NOT JUST FOR BATS

Scientists are discovering that more and more animals use echolocation. A variety of mammals are sensitive to ultrasound, including rats, hamsters, dormice, and marmosets. The long, twitching whiskers and large, flexible pinnae (outer ears) of these animals help them with echolocation by effectively collecting sound.

The shrew hears in part through echolocation, which it uses to hunt.

Common tree shrew, facing page

Songbirds

(Suborder: Passeres)

Songbirds and people hear pretty much the same musical notes. Yet, in a way, birds have hearing superior to ours. With very rapid notes, they can distinguish pitch (how high or low a sound is) better than we can. And birds can hear and respond to a song about ten times faster than humans. Their eardrums are also stronger. Loud and continuous noise can damage mammals' ears, but it seems impossible to deafen birds this way.

Take a look at the songbirds' ears. Where are they? Mostly hidden. The middle and inner ears of birds are very similar to those of mammals. But instead of the fleshy outer ears we have, birds have a tiny opening covered with feathers on either side of their head. No big, protruding ears means a sleeker body line for flight.

Hearing is the most important sense for birds. They can hear and respond to songs and calls of their own species, as well as many other noises. For the most part, songs claim territory, like a musical "No Trespassing Allowed!" sign. Other songs are used for courtship ("Be my mate!"), or alarm ("Predator nearby!"), or finding food ("Look! Worms!"). Some species can mimic other birds and even humans. Parrots, budgies, mynahs, magpies, crows, and starlings are famous for imitating the human voice and for whistling. The ability to mimic relies on acute and selective hearing.

Blue jay

BABY TALK

When newly hatched birds were kept in sound-proof cages until a certain age, they could still produce the sounds of their species and answer other birds' sounds correctly. This ability is instinctive, rather than learned. Can a human baby understand human speech if no one speaks to it and it never hears people talk? No. Every child learns from hearing others speak.

Bird songs often serve to warn others that a predator lurks nearby.

Cardinal, facing page

Dogs

(Canis familiaris)

Chow chow

ogs can hear a thunderstorm miles off. They can detect approaching visitors well before they knock on the door. They can hear small animals scurrying through brambles a considerable distance away. Many dogs can even distinguish the sound of their owner's car from the sound of other cars! These feats are possible because dogs have an extraordinarily acute sense of hearing.

Dog ears come in all shapes and sizes—pointy, shaped like tear drops, tulip-shaped, and just plain floppy. All forms of dog ears can hear far better than humans. Breeds with erect ears, like German shepherds and foxhounds, can hear best of all. When these pointy-eared pooches hear a noise, they prick up their ears and cock their heads to one side to locate the direction of the sound. Their wide-open ears act as effective antennae that can be turned to zero in on faint sounds. Dogs with floppy ears have a less acute sense of hearing since their ear flaps muffle incoming sound waves.

But whatever the shape and size of their ears, dogs hear sounds that are not only too distant for humans to hear, but also those that are too high in frequency. Dogs will respond to a pitch of 30,000 hertz, whereas very few humans hear sounds above 20,000 hertz. (Remember, frequency is measured in hertz.) These facts help explain the mysterious "silent" dog whistle. Puff into one of these, and you will hear nothing. Your dog, however, will hear a piercing blast over a half a mile away!

EAR SERVICE

Most people are familiar with guide dogs for the blind, but few know about dogs for the deaf, called hearing ear dogs. These dogs are trained to be helpers and companions to deaf people. Hearing ear dogs alert their owners when alarm clocks go off, doorbells ring, oven timers buzz, and tea kettles whistle. They even let deaf parents know when their baby is crying. Hearing ear dogs make it possible for deaf people to live more worry-free, independent lives.

All dogs have keen hearing, but breeds with pointy ears hear best of all.

Shetland sheepdog, facing page

Dolphins

(Delphinus delphis)

Like bats, these intelligent aquatic mammals use echolocation to interpret sound and orient themselves to their surroundings. Even humans use echolocation—an electronic version, that is, called sonar, for Sound Navigation Ranging. But dolphins do it naturally; they send out a series of clicks or ticking noises that travel through the water and then bounce off objects as echoes. The time it takes for an echo to return and the direction the echo comes from tell the dolphin the object's location.

Dolphins listen for these sounds with more than just their ears, which appear as tiny slits on either side of the head. Dolphins also use their lower jaws to receive sound and direct it to the inner ear and nerve centers. The lower jaw for hearing? Yes, because it is filled with an oily substance perfect for conducting vibrations. In one experiment, a blindfolded dolphin located an underwater sound transmitter, then placed its jaw against the speaker and kept it there for a long time—listening with its jaw, not its ears!

While cruising underwater, dolphins scan their general surroundings by sending out low frequencies, or wavelengths, of sound. Echoes from these sounds give dolphins "the big picture" of their environment. When zeroing in on an object, they transmit high frequencies of clicking sounds—as many as several hundred per second!—for a clearer, more accurate picture. Researchers are studying dolphins in the hope of developing electronic sonar and radar devices to help sightless people to "see."

SAY WHAT?

Do dolphins talk? According to some zoologists (scientists who study animals), dolphins communicate with each other using sequences of clicks, squeaks, whines, and other sounds. While traveling in schools, they may stop and have "discussions" about their surroundings and the best route to take around obstacles.

Dolphins send out scouts to explore an area and report back to the group.

Bottle-nosed dolphin, above and facing page

OILbirds

(Steatornis caripensis)

Deep inside the pitch black caverns of the South American jungle lives a peculiar creature called an oilbird. The oilbird's claim to fame is that it is one of the only birds in the entire world that uses echolocation—and it is a good thing that it does! The caves that the oilbird inhabits are so dark that eyesight is useless. The oilbird must depend solely on echolocation to navigate itself through the long, rocky passages of its cave home.

As the oilbird swoops through its unlit cave, it emits a series of low-frequency sounds, which humans hear as clicks. The sound waves of these "clicks" ricochet off nearby objects back to the bird's ears. The oilbird can then detect the presence of dangerous obstacles by analyzing the time delay between the initial "clicks" and the returning echoes. The longer the time delay, the farther away the object. But if the echoes return very quickly—look out! It means an obstacle is straight ahead, and the oilbird must hastily whoosh in the opposite direction to avoid a head-on collision.

Unlike bats, oilbirds do not use echolocation to find food. Rather, once out in the moonlit jungle, these nocturnal creatures rely on their keen sense of vision to locate the fruit they feed on. Echolocation is mostly helpful to oilbirds because it enables them to roost and nest in the total darkness of caves.

FRUGIVOROUS FEATHERED FRIENDS

The oilbird's snazzy sonar does more than enable them to navigate through the dark caves in which they live. It is also the reason they can be frugivorous (meaning they eat only fruit). Most birds cannot feed their young fruit because on such a diet nestlings grow more slowly and so are exposed to predators for a longer period of time. However, oilbirds can take full advantage of the abundant jungle fruit supply because their young are nestled in the high crevices inside caves, safe from predators.

Oilbirds use echolocation to navigate in the dark caves where they build their nests.

Oilbird, above and facing page

Monkeys

(Order: Primata)

Proboscis monkey

Monkeys' ears aren't very different from other mammals' ears. In general, they have excellent hearing. Monkeys make and understand complex acoustic signals: they scream, chatter, hoot, and grunt to communicate with each other. Like humans, monkeys are sociable animals. They live in tight-knit groups and must listen to and understand each other to survive.

Infant monkeys spend a long time with their mothers learning the many sounds used by their species. Yet even very young monkeys have calls to get attention or show distress. The infant vervet (or green monkey) has at least five distress calls when separated from its mother. The calls vary in frequency (remember low frequency and high frequency?) and intensity (decibel level).

The adult vervet monkey uses different cries of alarm for different dangers. If the cry warns of a ground-dwelling predator approaching—a leopard or a lion, for example—the monkeys climb the nearest tree. What do they do when they hear the eagle alarm call? They look up, then quickly seek cover in a nearby bush. What if they hear the unique "chatter" that alerts them to a snake? They look down at the ground—then they may actually mob the snake as a group and kill it.

Certain alarm calls make it hard to locate the caller. This makes sense: a caller that leads a predator to it won't last long. But other calls—mating calls, for example—make it easy for the caller to be located, as you might guess. How do monkeys figure out where the caller is? Three cues help: frequency, intensity, and the time the call arrives at each ear. It arrives sooner by a few milliseconds in the ear closer to the sound.

RIGHT-EARED?

Some monkeys listen better with their right ear than their left. Right ear advantage might mean the left half (or hemisphere) of the brain is dominant (stronger). That's the half of the brain that controls language in humans.

Monkeys have different warning calls for different predators. Here, a monkey warns its group of an approaching eagle.

Douc langur, facing page

34

SEALS

(Families: Phocidae and Otariidae)

What happens to a seal's ear when it dives into the water? The channel to its eardrum is closed by water pressure. A pocket of air is trapped inside which acts like a tiny drum, picking up vibrations from the seawater. As a result, seals have excellent underwater hearing. When scientists dangled bells underwater in one experiment, seals immediately came to investigate the noise.

Like dolphins, seals use echolocation to hunt and navigate underwater. Seals give off a series of clicks when they hunt. The clicks then bounce off the fish and lead the seal to its meal. Echolocation works so well that seals can hunt in total darkness.

Seals make other noises besides clicks. They have over thirty underwater calls, each with a different meaning—defending territory, aggression, submission, and mating, to name a few. On land, mother seals and their pups yell and cry at one another across the ice. As the pups grow up, they stop crying, much as human babies learn to talk, and begin to imitate the sounds of the adults around them. Sometimes seals even try to imitate humans. When one folk singer sang a tune called "Seal Song" to a group of seals, one of them "sang" back!

Galapagos fur seal

SEA EARS

Ages ago, some land mammals returned to the sea. At some point on this long evolutionary path, they lost their external ears—a sleek head makes a better swimmer. But sea lions and fur seals kept their outer ears, the only sea mammals to do so. Other evolutionary developments in the aquatic ear include a smaller, thicker eardrum and a very narrow auditory canal. Next time you are in the bath tub, dunk your head under and listen to the water running. Human hearing underwater is pretty good, but not as good as a seal's.

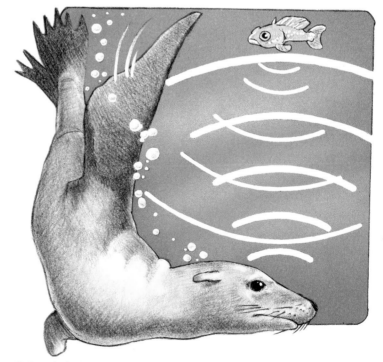

Like dolphins, seals use echolocation to hunt and navigate underwater.

Cape fur seal, facing page

Elephants

African elephant

Elephants really get down with sound—way down. These giant creatures are able to make and hear extremely low-frequency sound, called infrasound. (*Infra* means below.) These sounds are too low for humans to hear. For this reason, elephant behavior has seemed very mysterious to us. For no apparent reason, roaming elephants may suddenly freeze in their tracks and fall silent. Or a group of peaceful elephants at a watering hole may suddenly raise their heads in unison, then stampede off as if their lives depended on it. Until recently, scientists couldn't explain this mysterious behavior. It seemed that elephants communicated through some kind of telepathy, or "mind waves."

Recent experiments using sensitive microphones and recording devices have solved the mystery. Elephants use infrasound to communicate with each other over long distances. They produce these low-frequency calls by vibrating air through their nasal passages past a vocal chord. The vibrating air then travels up to the elephant's forehead, where it vibrates under the skin. These low, rumbling calls can travel as far as $2^1/_2$ miles, even through thick jungle vegetation that would block higher frequency sounds. In this way, distant groups of elephants can alert each other to the presence of danger or water or food. Though humans can't hear the infrasound calls of elephants, we can sometimes feel the deep vibrations, like distant thunder.

COOL IT

Elephants also use their ears to cool off. Since they have no sweat glands, when they are too hot they hold their ears out away from their heads and flap them slowly back and forth. This cools the blood in the vessels in the ears, which then circulates back to the rest of the body and helps the elephant keep its cool. Lucky for the elephant it has such large ear flaps—the largest in the animal kingdom.

When elephants produce infrasound, their foreheads vibrate.

Elephant, facing page

OW1S

(Order: Strigiformes)

Although it has keen vision, an owl can zero in on prey using only its sense of hearing. Even on the darkest nights and at distances as great as half a mile, owls can find the exact location of prey. Owl ears are two long slits on either side of the head, covered by flaps of feathered skin. Owls can move their ear flaps to help them pinpoint the source of a sound. The flaps protect an owl's inner ear and funnel sound into the ear cavity.

Most owls have asymmetrical (uneven) ear cavities located in slightly different positions on either side of their head. Each of the ears works independently. Sounds reach one ear before the other, sending different pieces of information about the prey's location and distance to the owl's brain. The ears of the saw-whet owl are extremely sensitive to sound, but so asymmetrical that this little owl's head looks lopsided!

The process owls use to locate sounds is called triangulation. The "triangle" is formed with the owl's ears as the base angles and the sound source as the third angle. The owl's ears send the information to its brain, which judges the distance and location of a sound source relative to the ears' position. Owls also use their flexible necks to help them fix on the sound source. In fact, they can turn their heads three-quarters of a circle.

Barn owl

FOOLED YOU

An owl's pointy "ear" tufts have nothing at all to do with hearing. They are only showy feathers, called plumage, that stick up on either side of some owls' heads. They were probably misnamed ear tufts because they look like ears.

Owls hear high-frequency sound best, such as the squeak of a mouse—even a half mile away.

Long-eared owl, facing page

Whales

(Order: Cetacea)

Humpback whale

A whale's ears appear as two quarter-inch slits on either side of its enormous head. Some scientists believe that whales, like dolphins, use the oil-filled channels in their lower jaws to receive and conduct sound. Whales are mammals, not fish, and their inner ears are very similar to ours (though much bigger!). But their ears have some special features suited to their underwater environment. The middle and inner parts of a whale's ear are set in a rigid, dense bone called the tympanic bulla. This heavy dome helps sound carried through water (which is denser than air) to travel through the auditory canal to the auditory nerves and then to the brain. Whales' large brains are highly developed to interpret sound.

And just what do whales hear in the murky depths? Plenty. Whales produce a wide range of sounds, some of which humans can hear: moans, chirps, grunts, and whale songs. Humpback whales are the opera singers of the deep, able to produce 21 sounds with 84 variations! The sounds are phrases, and each whale seems to put the phrases together differently depending on the message it's sending. Whales can communicate with each other over hundreds of underwater miles. Yet some whale sounds vibrate right past the human ear, too low or too high in frequency to be detected. The very low-frequency sound whales make is called infrasound; the very high-frequency sound is called ultrasound.

Hearing is essential to whales' survival. Since visibility is limited underwater, whales depend on their ears to "see." Like dolphins and seals, they use echolocation to navigate and hunt.

STRANDED

History has recorded thousands of whale strandings on beaches. Until recently, however, the reason for this was a mystery. Now, some cetologists (scientists who study whales) believe that whales beach themselves when their echolocation system is disrupted. Shallow, muddy waters or sudden changes in the Earth's magnetic field can confuse a whale's ability to echolocate with accuracy.

Why do whales beach themselves? Probably because their echolocation system has been "jammed."

Orca, facing page

SIMPLE TO COMPLEX

Eyes in the animal kingdom vary from very simple light sensors to highly complex, specialized eyes. Whatever the type of eye, all sight is possible because of a substance called **visual pigment**. When light strikes the visual pigment in an eye, the pigment changes chemically. This change causes an electrical signal to be sent from the eye to the brain through nerves. The cells containing the visual pigment are **photosensitive**, which means they are sensitive to light.

The very simplest eyes are nothing more than a collection of photosensitive cells. Some animals, like the starfish, have photosensitive cells all over their bodies, but they cannot focus on distinct shapes like humans can. Other animals have basic eyes that have a **lens** as well as photosensitive cells. The lens helps the eye to gather more light and projects it onto a group of photosensitive cells behind the lens. This group of cells is called the **retina**.

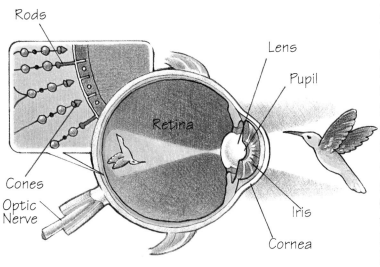

Rods

Lens

Pupil

Retina

Cones

Optic Nerve

Iris

Cornea

The human eye

For an animal to see a tree, a rock, or some other image, the lens in its eye must focus an image on the retina. Also, the retina must have a lot of photosensitive cells in it. In many animals, these photosensitive cells have special functions to help the eye see under different conditions. The retina of *your* eye, for example, is made up of **rods** and **cones**, groups of cells named for their shapes. Rods detect dim light and record images in black and white. Animals with excellent night vision have large numbers of rods. Cones detect color in bright light. Human eyes have 6 million cones, so we can see many beautiful colors.

The most advanced eyes, like yours, can see things that are both close and far away. To accomplish this, the eye must be able to change the shape of its lens. Specialized muscles push or pull on the lens to make it fat and round (to see things up close) or thin and flat (to see things at a distance). The lens changes shape because it needs to bend light coming in your eye so that it falls on your retina. The ability to focus on an image, to see it sharply without blurry edges, is called **visual acuity**, or **resolving power**.

In front of the lens of advanced eyes sits the **iris**, a flexible set of muscles that expands and contracts to open and close the hole that lets light into the eye. The iris is the colored part of the eye. The hole in the iris is called the **pupil**. The iris shrinks or enlarges the pupil to control the amount of light that enters the eye. In very low light, the pupil grows big to let in as much light as possible. In very bright light, it contracts to a small hole.

ELECTROMAGNETIC SPECTRUM

Different colors are made up of light waves of different lengths, or frequencies. The snake can see very low-frequency light waves, called **infrared**, which produces heat. The honey bee can see very high-frequency light waves, called **ultraviolet**. The full range of light frequencies is called the **electromagnetic spectrum**.

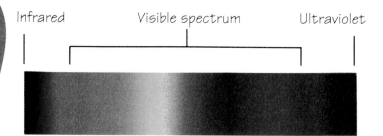

Infrared   Visible spectrum   Ultraviolet

The range of colors humans can see is only a tiny slice of the full spectrum. We cannot see infrared or ultraviolet rays, or those light frequencies beyond them.

Compound Eyes

Insects and crustaceans (such as crabs and lobsters) have eyes that are made up of hundreds of little lenses grouped together, each backed by its own photosensitive cells. These are called **compound eyes.** When a fly sees you with its compound eyes, it does not see only one image of you: it probably sees hundreds of the same image of you. Compound eyes cannot focus clearly on an object, but they are very effective in detecting motion, especially in dim light.

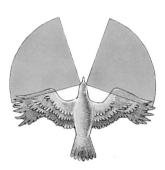

Most birds have monocular vision only.

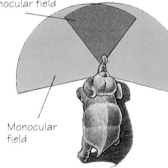

An elephant's monocular visual fields overlap to give the animal binocular vision over its trunk.

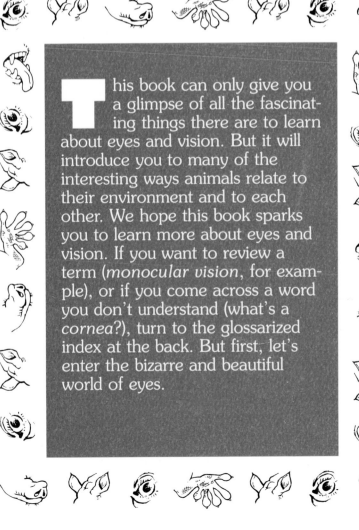

The compound eye of a dragonfly

Monocular and Binocular Vision

Many animals have eyes on the sides of their heads that scan the horizon on each side and move independently of each other. This is called **monocular vision**. In the sea horse, for example, one eye can look up while the other looks down, one right while the other looks left. This is very important to animals that need to watch out for predators—they can see more of what is going on around them than we can. The area each eye scans is called its **visual field**.

Humans and many other species have two eyes on the front of their faces that always move together in the same direction. The result is that both eyes see the same image. This is called **binocular vision**. This can be very helpful, for two reasons. First, since both eyes see the same image, together they see it much more clearly than one eye would alone. Second, since both eyes converge toward nearby objects, the eyes are better able to judge distance. This is called **depth perception**. To see how important depth perception is to you, put an eye patch over one eye and walk around the room. Do you have trouble telling how far away objects are?

This book can only give you a glimpse of all the fascinating things there are to learn about eyes and vision. But it will introduce you to many of the interesting ways animals relate to their environment and to each other. We hope this book sparks you to learn more about eyes and vision. If you want to review a term (*monocular vision*, for example), or if you come across a word you don't understand (what's a *cornea*?), turn to the glossarized index at the back. But first, let's enter the bizarre and beautiful world of eyes.

STarfish

(Class: Asteroidea)

Although they are not fish, most people call these sea stars by their common name—starfish. Marine biologists, scientists who study sea life, named these creatures "asteroids," which is Greek for "like a star." Starfish have photosensitive cells all over their bodies that react to light. Imagine being able to sense light from head to toe, just as your sense of touch covers your whole body. In the same way, starfish have light receptors from tip to tip of their many arms. They cannot, however, see distinct shapes and objects, like fish or rocks.

Near the tip of their arms, which usually number five, is a place called the eyespot, or optic cushion. If you shine a light on this eyespot, the starfish moves its arm. If you shine a light on the entire starfish, some types retreat but most creep forward. Almost every species of starfish (and there are more than two thousand!) moves in a predictable way.

The starfish does not really know it reacts to light anymore than it knows that it has just started to move. This is because it doesn't have a brain. Instead, its photosensitive cells connect to nerve cells. These nerves, in turn, send a message to the arm muscles: "Get going!" Its muscles react automatically (a reflex), and the starfish begins to creep over the rocks and sand of its watery home.

Ochre starfish

CLAM UP

A month-old starfish can devour more than four dozen young clams in less than a week! But if they cannot see them, how do starfish find their prey? During its ocean-floor patrol, the starfish uses its sense of touch to "see" food—a clam, for example. The suction power of the starfish's arms pries open the clam's shell. The starfish then positions its stomach right on top of the opened clam and starts munching. No wonder fishermen who harvest clams, oysters, and mussels want to keep starfish out of their fishing beds!

EYESPOT
TENTACLE
TUBE FEET

The arms of the starfish are covered with photosensitive cells and tipped with an eyespot. The tube feet are used for walking and for prying open the shells of molluscs.

Starfish, facing page

SCallops

(Chiamys opercularis)

What has one hundred unblinking, bright blue eyes that sit around the rim of its shell? The scallop, of course. The scallop is a shellfish, a small, soft-bodied creature that hides inside its distinctive fan-shaped shell. Its tiny eyes alternate with tentacles in two rows all around its shell. What makes the scallop's blue eyes so bright? The thin mirror-like lenses of their eyes reflect the blue of the surrounding sea, making them sparkle like shining sapphires. With eyes pointing in every direction, the scallop keeps a careful watch on its underwater world.

The main thing the scallop is on the lookout for is the starfish—humans aren't the only ones who find scallops delicious! Luckily for the scallop, it is not as helpless as it looks. Although its eyes probably do not see distinct shapes, they are sensitive to movement. If so much as the shadow of a starfish passes over the scallop, the two sides of its shell snap shut. When a starfish approaches, the scallop springs into action. The scallop is an excellent swimmer. Its method of locomotion (movement) is to shoot water out from between its valves and leap forward. With its alert eyes and ability to dart away, the scallop can escape the starfish.

Scallops are sociable creatures and gather together by the thousands in clean sand beds. They live in warm seas throughout the world.

Deep sea scallop

HEAD IN THE SAND

The scallop is a member of the mollusc family. Its cousins include the octopus, slug, oyster, and cockle. The cockle spends much of its time nestled beneath the sand. A safe place to hide, but how does the creature watch out for hunters, especially hunters that dig? The cockle has small eyes that sit on top of stalks. It can raise its eyes right out of the sand and look around, just as if its eyes were a periscope on a submarine.

The scallop shoots water out from between its valves and leaps forward to escape its main predator, the starfish.

Queen scallop, facing page

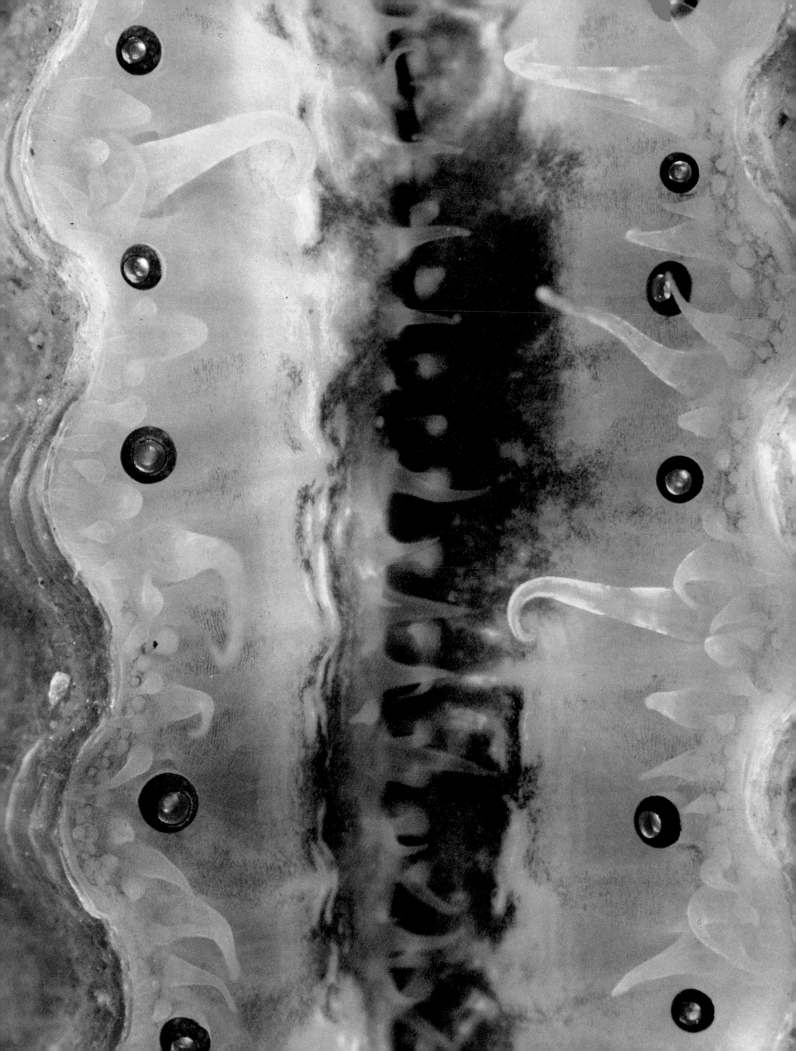

SP iDe *rs*

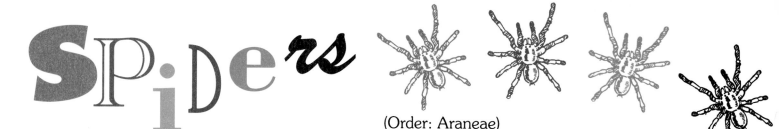

(Order: Araneae)

A wolf spider slowly creeps toward its insect prey—then suddenly darts forward, lunges, and bites its victim. Wolf spiders are hunting spiders, dependent on their eyes for survival, unlike their web-building cousins. Web-spinners do not have keen eyesight. They sit and wait for the movement of prey caught in their webs, then follow the vibrations to attack. Hunters such as wolf, fisher, and jumping spiders, however, sight prey with their sharp eyes—all eight of them.

Most spiders have eight eyes, arranged in pairs in two rows on their heads. Unlike the compound eyes of insects, spider eyes have a single lens. One pair, the principal eyes, can move and focus on objects because they have retinas. The other three pairs, called secondary eyes, do not move, but they take in more light than the principal eyes.

The principal and secondary eye pairs serve different purposes. In jumping spiders, the secondary eyes react first, detecting movement. The spider's legs then begin to move and it turns to face the movement source. The secondary eyes then send messages to the brain about the object's distance, and the spider begins creeping forward. Next, the principal eyes scan the object in sight to determine what it is. If it's an insect, the spider will attack. In the hunter spider *Olios*, each pair of secondary eyes sees a different field of vision—forward and down, upwards, and to the rear sides. Many spiders even have eyes that see behind their heads.

Hammock spider

ANCESTRAL ARACHNIDS

Did you know that spiders are not insects? They're officially called arachnids, along with scorpions, ticks, and mites. Arachnids are animals without backbones (invertebrates) that have four pairs of legs. The arachnid ancestors of today's spiders probably had both compound and single-lens eyes. Most likely, the spider's principal eyes evolved from basic eyes, and the three secondary eye pairs came from a splitting up of compound eyes. The earliest spiders were probably all web builders and did not depend much on their eyes for their survival. But with evolutionary changes, some spiders ventured away from the web and developed larger, more sensitive eyes and better acuity for hunting.

Most spiders have eight eyes arranged in two rows on their heads. One pair of eyes can even see behind their heads.

Jumping spider, facing page

Beetles

(Order: Coleoptera)

There are a quarter of a million types of beetles—so many, in fact, that these insects make up 80 percent of all species on Earth. Beetles live in jungles, cities, deserts, lakes, and just about everywhere else except the open sea and the icy continent of Antarctica.

With so many types of beetles, it's no surprise there are many different kinds of beetle eyes. There are small-eyed beetles and beetles whose eyes are so big they take up most of their head. Certain beetles can see colors, and a few can even sense infrared light that humans cannot see. Some beetles, like the whirligig, have eyes divided into lobes that allow them to see above and below at the same time. Some beetles see best in bright light, others in dim light. There are even beetles with no eyes at all that live deep in the soil and in caves, where no light ever shines. They detect passing meals (smaller insects) with long hairs that can feel the air move beside them.

Like other insects, beetles have compound eyes made up of hundreds of tiny lenses that aim light toward the beetle's retina. When light hits *your* retina, it forms a clear image that is upside down. Inside the beetle's eye, the image is right side up, but it is out of focus.

Elder borer beetle

LIGHT UP

Fireflies are not flies at all, but beetles that make their own light. And glowworms are not worms, either. They are beetles, too—wingless, female firefly beetles. Beetles such as fireflies are one of the few animals able to produce light. This ability is known as bioluminescence (bio means life, and luminescence is a fancy word for light). Different species of fireflies flash their lights differently. One type can even produce two different colors! The beetles' flashing "code" is their way of recognizing members of their own species. All young fireflies can light up—it's part of their mating behavior—but not all adults can.

With a quarter of a million species of beetle, it's no surprise there are many sizes, shapes, and types of beetle eyes.

52

Convergent lady beetles, facing page

Seahorses

(Genus: *Hippocampus*)

What looks like a horse but is actually a fish? The unusual sea horse. This interesting creature has excellent monocular vision. Its two eyes move independently of each other. One eye may be looking straight ahead, searching the underwater forest for a tasty snack, while the other checks behind to make sure no morsel has escaped notice. Each of the sea horse's eyes can look up, down, forward, backward, or simply straight ahead. The eyes protrude (bug out), which adds to the creature's strange appearance.

Like other fishes, the sea horse has no eyelids—which is why it sleeps with its eyes open. As it vanishes into a jungle of underwater plants, the sea horse's eyes keep a vigilant watch on the changing underwater environment. But the sea horse itself is difficult to spot. Some sea horses can even change their own color when light conditions in the water change. They can match a lighter or darker environment and blend in with grasses, sponges, and coral.

Its eyes make the sea horse a spectacular hunter of its favorite food, small crustaceans. Like the African chameleon, whose eyes move in the same independent way, the sea horse remains still and camouflaged in the seaweed before darting out to snatch a meal. Sea horses have a hearty appetite. A tiny newborn can eat up to 3,000 crustacean larvae in a morning! When the sea horse is not trying to escape becoming someone else's meal, it moves up and down in the ocean depths, as if it were riding an elevator.

Caribbean sea horse

DEEP DARK SEA

It is more difficult to see underwater than on land, as you may have noticed the last time you opened your eyes in a lake or swimming pool. Underwater light is scattered, and darker in the daytime that it would be on the surface. Like land animals that hunt at night, a fish's eye must collect enough light for its brain to process images. Fishes' retinas have large groups of rods bundled together, giving their eyes better vision in their dark underwater environment.

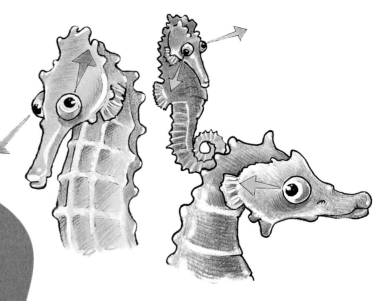

The sea horse's protruding eyes work independently of each other and can look up, down, sideways, backward, or simply straight ahead.

Atlantic lined sea horse, facing page

FoUr-EyEd FiSh

(Anableps anableps)

This small freshwater fish resembles a minnow—except for its eyes, of course. The four-eyed fish actually has only two eyes, but each eye is divided in two by a band of skin. It spends most of its time just under the surface of the water, the top half of each eye peering above the waterline. With the top part of the eye, it watches for bird predators; with its lower eye, which is adapted for underwater vision, it watches for prey. When the four-eyed fish spots a meal, it dives down to catch it, then zips back up to the surface.

Though divided in two, the *Anableps'* eye has only a single, oval-shaped lens. But this lens does double duty, acting like bifocal (two-lensed) goggles that aid sight both in and out of water.

The *Anableps* was originally thought to be the only true four-eyed fish. But another fish, *Bathylchnops exilis*, was recently discovered in the deep waters of the Pacific, where it lives as far down as 3,000 feet. At that level, light is the blue of twilight on a winter evening. Millions of rods in the *Bathylchnops'* retina make it sensitive to the dim light. Wide vision and keen sight help this quickly darting fish catch its prey. The *Bathylchnops'* two eyes are bifocal; the lower lens of each eye gazes downwards and has its own retina. Behind these small eyes are two even smaller eye-like organs (which lack retinas). They probably serve to bend light into the pair of large eyes. Further research may reveal why this deep-sea creature needs two eyes . . . or rather, four . . . or is it six?

SURFER DUDE

The four-eyed blenny (*Dialommus fuscus*) lives on the rocky coast of the Galapagos Islands. Its eyes are divided in two by a vertical (up and down) band. It eats small crustaceans when it leaves the rocks at low tide. Then this 3-inch-long surfer rides the crest of a wave safely back into a crevice.

With eyes divided in two by a band of skin, the four-eyed fish uses aerial vision to watch for predators and underwater sight to search for prey.

Anableps, *above and facing page*

Dragonflies

(Order: Odonata)

If you've ever been around a lake or a pond on a summer day, chances are you've seen dragonflies darting about—flying in one direction, hovering, then darting off again. What are they so busy doing? Hunting—what else?—for food like flies, gnats, mosquitoes, and even butterflies. The dragonfly's large compound eyes sit on either side of its head. These eyes are keenly adapted to seeing movement, especially of small objects like flying insects.

Most critters in the insect world have compound eyes (remember the beetle?). Magnified, they look something like a honeycomb. A compound eye is made up of hundreds of tiny lenses, all pointing in a different direction. Each lens acts like an individual eye. If a dragonfly were looking at you, for instance, it would see hundreds of tiny images of you. Compound eyes are very sensitive to movement. This is because the movement is seen by each and every lens. If a friend waves at you, your single-lens eyes see one motion. The dragonfly would see a flutter of movements as the wave was projected on each and every one of its lenses.

Compound eyes can't move like our eyes. Instead, a dragonfly "scans" its environment without moving its eyes or its head. Because dragonflies attack their prey from below, they need to see best at an angle looking forward and up. This is why the lenses in the upper portion of a dragonfly's eye are larger; they have greater acuity (ability to focus) for hunting. It's interesting that helicopters—which look like mechanical dragonflies—tilt forward in fast flight, and their domes point up, just like dragonfly eyes.

Common sympetrum

cone through which light is focused

light sensitive cells

lens

QUICK EYES

Dragonflies hunt on the fly and often eat their prey without bothering to land. Their compound eyes are therefore adapted to perceive quick movement and direction. An insect that flies across a dragonfly's visual field sets off a flicker pattern of light signals across the eye. The dragonfly's brain is sensitive to the exact timing of these signals.

A dragonfly's compound eyes are made up of hundreds of tiny lenses. Each acts like an individual eye. Together, they send a mosaic-like image to the insect's brain.

Aeschna cyanea, facing page

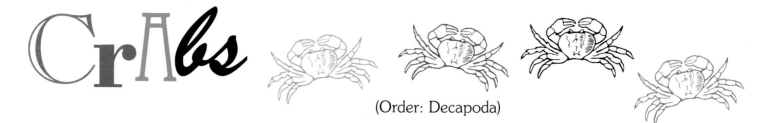

CrAbs

(Order: Decapoda)

Horned-eye ghost crab

As a rule, crabs have excellent vision. The eye of the horseshoe crab (*Limulus*) evolved many thousands of years ago, making it one of the most ancient eyes in the animal kingdom. Like insects, horseshoe crabs have compound eyes. These sit on top of its armored shell and can see as clearly at night as during the day. Imagine if you stepped out on a dark, moonless evening and could see your neighborhood in almost as much detail as if the sun were shining brightly. This is how well the horseshoe crab can see its nighttime world. It uses ultraviolet light to see when the sky is dark. Incredibly, the crab's brain sends signals to its eyes at dusk and at dawn to increase the creature's vision in dim light.

The horseshoe crab does not use its sharp eyesight to find food, as you might expect. Instead, it uses its vision to select a mate from among the crowds of crabs who gather on the sandy shores of the eastern United States.

The eyes of the ghost crab (*Ocypode ceratophthalmus*) perch on top of thin stalks on the crab's head, enabling the crab to see in all directions. Each eye is made up of thousands of photosensitive cells. These cells help orient the crab towards the sun and, scientists suspect, also towards the dimmer light of the moon.

DANGER IN SIGHT

Fiddler crabs, like ghost crabs, are very alert to their environment. This helps them to escape water birds like egrets who might be looking for a tasty bite of crab. The Indian fiddler crab can sense an egret at a distance of 25 feet (about 8 meters) and will not wait for the bird to come closer before it scurries off for cover. Deep-water and cave-dwelling crabs have less accurate eyesight. Touch and vibration are more important to them than good vision.

The horseshoe crab uses its vision not to find food but to choose a mate out of the crowd of crabs on the shore.

Sand crab, facing page

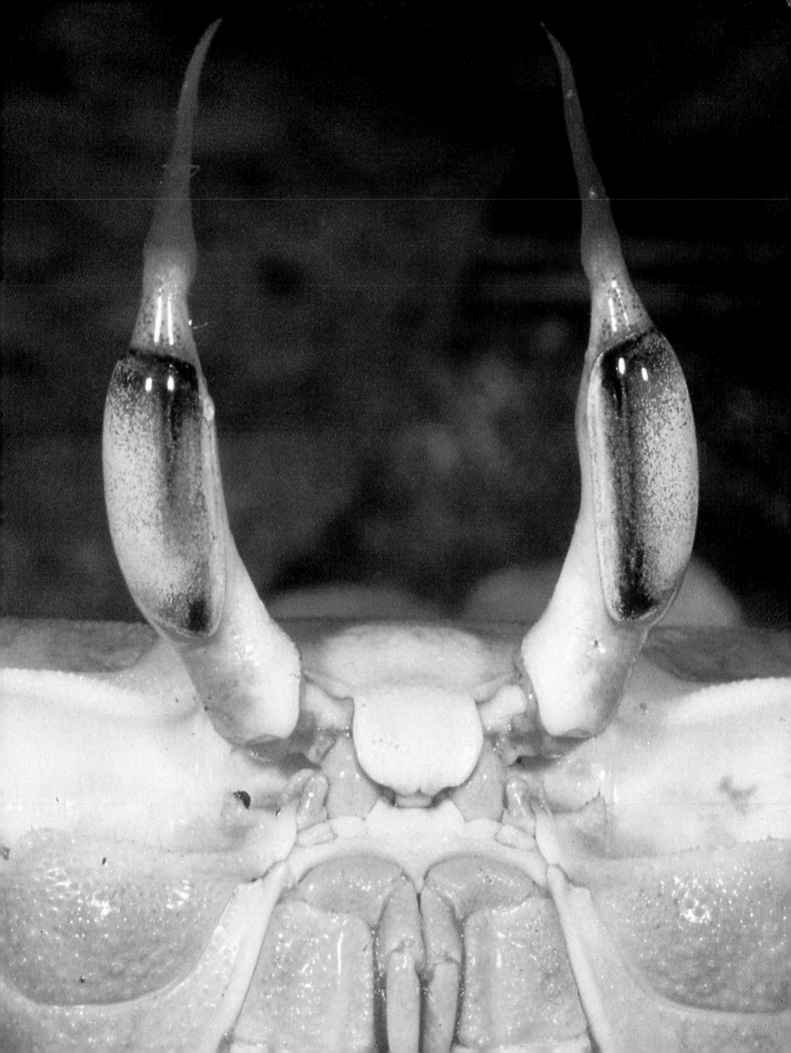

SNakes

(Order: Squamata)

Have you ever seen a snake blink? No—because they can't. Snakes have no eyelids. Their eyes are always open, even when they sleep. How are their eyes protected and cleansed? A thin transparent skin covers their eyes with a veil of lachrymal liquid, a technical term for tears.

Parrot snake

When the snake molts (sheds its skin), it sheds its eyecovers, too. At this point, they are no longer clear, but opaque, like a fogged up window. Sometimes the snake rubs itself against trees or rocks to help slough off the old skin. Sometimes it sheds its skin in one piece, like a child wiggling out of sleeper pajamas.

Vision is the dominant sense in snakes. It is very keen in all but burrowing types of snakes. The lens of the snake's eye focuses accurately within a somewhat limited range. Snakes that hunt by day have rounded pupils. Snakes that hunt at night have vertical, elliptical (oval) pupils, similar to those of a cat. Elliptical pupils admit or shut out light more efficiently than round pupils. Snake eyes are sensitive to even the slightest movements—such as those made by the small creatures that make up their diet.

P.S. Snakes are probably color-blind.

FEEL THE HEAT

How does a snake "see" to hunt in the dark? It senses heat. Pit vipers and rattlesnakes sense the infrared radiation given off by their warm-blooded prey. These "eyes" are the pit organs, two deep cavities located on the snake's head under and in front of the eyes. Heat-sensitive nerve fibers send messages to the snake's brain. In North America, other snakes with this infrared "vision" are the cottonmouth (water moccasin) and copperhead. Pythons and other distant relatives of pit vipers also have heat-sensitive pits. Instead of just one pair, though, they have many pits, sometimes more than a dozen, on scales bordering their mouths.

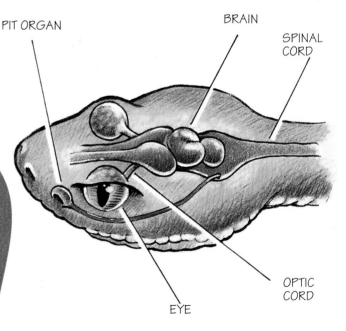

Many species of snakes have pit organs, cavities on their heads that sense tiny changes in temperature. These heat-sensitive organs help them detect the movement of warm-blooded prey.

62

Eye of Indian green tree snake, facing page

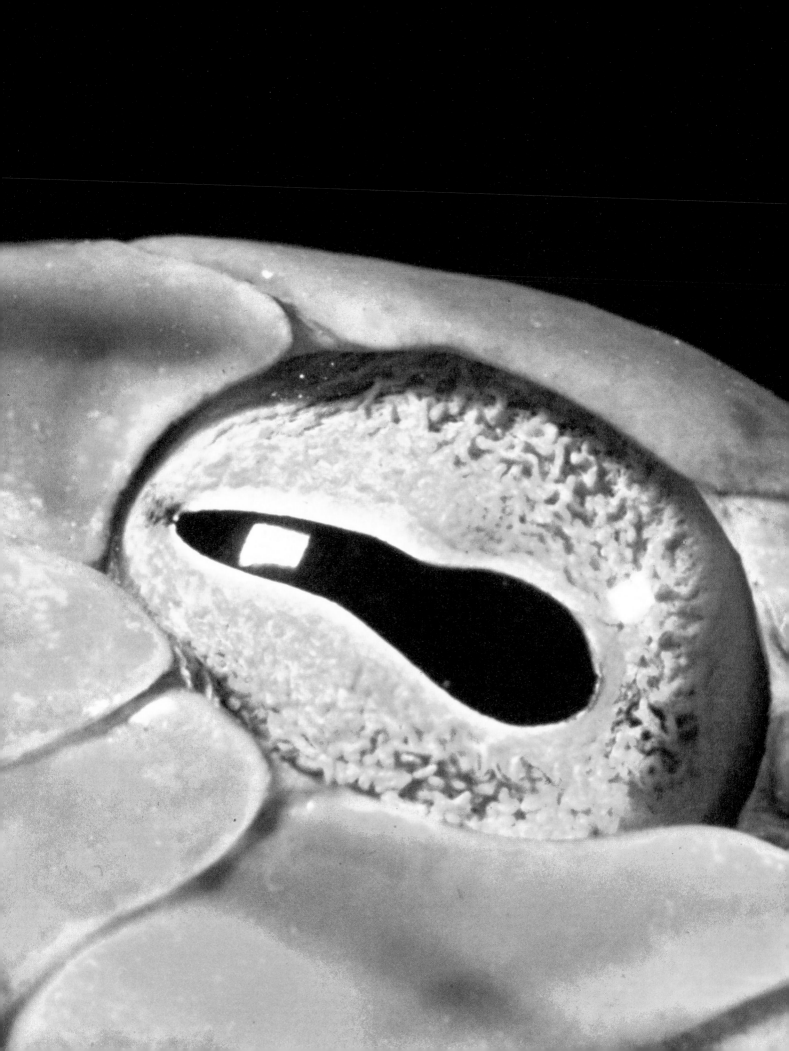

FrOGs

(Order: Salientia)

Green tree frog

Frogs sitting at the edge of a pond aren't waiting for a beautiful princess to come by and kiss them. No, they're waiting for food, and food in the frog world means insects. Frogs usually keep very still, always on the lookout for visual signals from assorted flying and crawling bugs and worms. Frog eyes respond well to light and to the movement of small passing objects—especially to their favorite passing objects: insects. Frogs will eat something only if it moves; they ignore motionless objects. In fact, one group of researchers could only get their frogs to eat if they served them wriggling worms by hand! Then they found an easier way. They put bits of hamburger on a lazy Susan turntable. The frogs snapped at the moving food as it spun by!

Frogs' large, bulging eyes give them a very wide field of vision. Each eye's field of vision overlaps with the other, giving the frog binocular vision and good depth perception (the ability to judge distance). Frogs estimate the size and location of moving prey before flashing their long sticky tongues to catch it. A frog will not try to catch an insect that's too far away. Instead, it turns its body toward the insect and waits until the prey is within "zapping zone"—the length of the frog's tongue and reach.

EYE STRIPES

The colored iris of a frog's eye, like yours, expands or contracts to enlarge or shrink the size of the pupil. This adjusts the amount of light that enters the eye. But the iris is also a camouflage device. Different frog species have irises of different colors. Often, these colors blend with a frog's facial pattern to help conceal the frog.

In some frog species, eye color is a camouflaging device. Markings on the frog's body, like stripes, may continue right through the iris.

Asiatic horned frog, facing page

Chameleons

(Family: Chamaeleonidae)

These lizards are among very few animals with both monocular and binocular vision. The chameleon's exceptional eyesight helps it spot the small insects that make up its diet (locusts are a favorite). Independently of each other, its two huge eyes scan the area for possible prey. Once the chameleon spies an insect with one eye, it turns its head and, now using binocular vision, focuses both eyes on the target. The chameleon then creeps toward its next meal, stopping when it comes within its long tongue's reach. (In some chameleons, that's as long as their body and tail combined.) Then—*ZAP!* The chameleon's sticky tongue shoots out to snatch the insect.

The chameleon aims and shoots its tongue straight ahead with amazing speed and accuracy. Then it withdraws its tongue and bunches it up inside its mouth, like a sweater pushed up at the sleeve. The chameleon depends on a lightning quick attack for its survival—if its tongue simply lolled out of its mouth, the insect would escape. But a fast tongue is not enough. The chameleon relies on its acute (sharp) vision to judge the distance and position of its prey.

Chameleons' powerful eyes are protected by thick scaly eyelids that are shaped like cones and cover the eyes at all times. How can the lizard see with its eyes closed? There is a small hole in the middle of each eyelid, over the iris. The chameleon looks out this tiny "window" to see.

BLENDING IN

Have you ever heard someone described as a "chameleon"? It means that person changes from situation to situation—just like the lizard. Responding to cues from light and temperature, chameleons can change the color of their skin. Usually chameleons assume colors that allow them to blend into their environment and hide from predators. But when fighting or threatened, they may display bold, brilliant colors—perhaps to "psyche out" their opponents. Most species of chameleons are found in Africa and Asia.

A chameleon spies an insect and—*ZAP!*—snatches it with its long sticky tongue.

Jackson's chameleon, facing page

DOGs
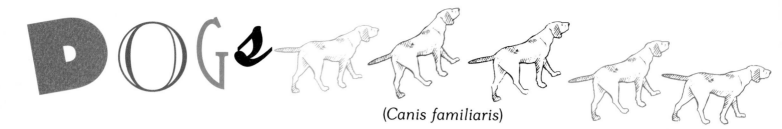

(Canis familiaris)

ost puppies are born blind, deaf, and totally helpless. A puppy's eyes are actually perfect at birth, but it takes about ten days for the eyelids to open. No one is exactly sure when puppies develop the full adult range of sight, but in most dogs it seems to be at about six weeks. That's also the usual time puppies are weaned and begin to bond with their human companions.

And just how well do adult dogs see? Not very, according to scientists who have studied dog vision. For starters, dogs are near-sighted and have astigmatism, which means distant objects appear blurry to them. Dogs are also partially color blind. They *can* see shades of blue and grey, but they confuse green, yellow, orange, and red as the same color. Dogs do, however, have excellent peripheral vision and are sensitive to motion. A dog will have no trouble spotting a rabbit bolting for cover out of the corner of its eye.

Of course, most dogs have a keen sense of smell to help make up for their mediocre vision. Even so, there are certain dogs known as "sight-hunting hounds," like greyhounds, Irish wolfhounds, and Afghans. These dogs are lean and swift, able not only to sight their prey but to pursue it with amazing speed. Sight-hunters are among the most ancient breeds of dogs. Pictures of them have even been found painted on the temples and tombs of Ancient Egypt.

Labrador retriever

GLOW IN THE DARK

Have you ever seen a dog's eyes shine when light hits them? Dogs, cats, and other animals that hunt at night have a reflecting layer behind their retinas. It acts like a piece of aluminum foil and reflects light back out of the eye, giving the animal better night vision.

Caught in the glare of headlights, a dog's eyes radiate an eerie yellow light. This is caused by the reflecting layer inside the animal's eye.

Husky eye, facing page

OCtoPus

(Octopus vulgaris)

The octopus is an extraordinary creature who has gotten a bad rap. Far from being the ferocious sea monster of sci-fi movies, the octopus is a very shy, intelligent creature. In fact, it has the largest brain of any invertebrate, which is an animal without a backbone. The octopus has eight tentacles (arm-like appendages) that help it crawl and swim and grasp food. Like its cousin the scallop, the octopus has a focusing lens in each eye that helps it both detect movement and judge distance. If several crabs are swimming nearby, the octopus will always make the right choice and grab the nearest one.

The octopus's good eyesight combined with its evolved brain allow it to learn simply by watching, rather than doing. When researchers train one octopus to do something, all the others pick up the behavior through observation. Some captive octopuses even figure out how to escape from their tanks.

In many animals, the ability to see color is linked to the ability to change color; animals that can camouflage themselves usually also can see a broad spectrum of colors. This is true of the octopus. The octopus changes color by squeezing pigment sacs located all over its body. Detecting rapid shifts in the hues around it, the octopus hides itself from predators in the nooks and crannies of underwater rocks.

GENTLE MONSTERS

Maybe you've seen horror movies in which gigantic squids fight with whales or squash submarines in their enormous tentacles. Although squids, cousins of the octopus, are much gentler in real life than in these movies, they do have an alarming appearance. This is partly due to their unusual eyes. Although they have one normal-looking eye, some squids also have a large tube-shaped eye with a yellow lens that points upward, giving it a wider field of vision.

The octopus has good depth perception, which means it can judge distance. If several crabs swim by, the octopus will always grab the nearest one.

Lesser octopus, facing page

OWLs

(Order: Strigiformes)

When it comes to sight, owls have the best bird's-eye view. No other birds can compete with an owl's ability to see in the dark *and* see great distances. No other birds have eyes as big in relation to their face and body size. Owls' wide eyes sit on the front of their flat faces, like ours do; like us, they have binocular vision. But unlike human eyes, owl eyes cannot move in their sockets. For peripheral vision, owls swivel their flexible necks as much as 270 degrees—about three-quarters of a circle.

Owl eyes are unique in many ways. Owls see clearly in very low light. This is because their retinas are packed with many light-sensitive rod cells and their pupils are exceptionally large, letting in lots of light. In fact, owl eyes gather light three to six times more efficiently than human eyes. Owls can also see details of objects at great distances. (Some owl species are even far-sighted; they see most clearly objects that are far away but have trouble focusing on what's up close.) Combined with their swift flight, owls' acute sight makes them extraordinary night hunters. They are able to spot— and pounce on—field mice and rabbits even when they're hidden by brush or darkness. Their acute sense of hearing also helps them hunt at night.

Because an owl's eyes are so important to its survival, it has developed ways to protect them. A clear layer called a nictitating membrane covers the eyes when an owl flies through dense brush or struggles with prey. This membrane also serves to clean the eye and the inside of the eyelids. Each eye has two lids, the upper one for blinking, the lower one for closing when the owl sleeps.

Barn owl

BRIGHT LIGHTS

The great horned owl has no trouble looking directly into a clear sky on a sunny day. It never squints, as we do in the glare of bright sunlight. In fact, it can stare straight at the sun without discomfort or damage to its eyes. This is because its pupils are vertical slits, similar to a cat's pupils, and don't admit as much light as round pupils like ours.

Because owl eyes cannot move in their sockets, owls have evolved flexible necks that can turn 270 degrees—three-quarters of a circle.

72

Great horned owl, facing page

Penguins

(Family: Spheniscidae)

King penguin

Penguins are birds who can't fly, but they can swim and dive with Olympic style. They hurtle into the freezing waters of the Antarctic Ocean to catch fish and crustaceans. They remain close to the surface and usually stay underwater for a minute or less—although Emperor penguins have been known to submerge themselves for nearly twenty minutes. Penguins have heavy bones and flippers instead of wings. Everything about them is equipped for diving.

The world a penguin sees is quite different from the world you see. This is because a penguin's eye is adapted perfectly for seeing under-water. When a penguin dives into the ocean, it sees its watery environment very sharply. The tough muscles around the iris make the penguins eye especially strong. Penguins also have good peripheral vision so they can watch out for underwater predators, such as the black and white orca (a type of whale). Visual pigments similar to those in fish eyes let the penguin see color, the seascape hues of violet, blue, and green. But that's not all. Penguins can see well into the ultraviolet range of the electromagnetic spectrum, beyond what is visible to humans.

CLOSE UP

With its unique flat cornea, the penguin's eye is adapted for excellent aquatic vision. It is able to see distinct shapes underwater and can focus on what's right under its beak. This comes in handy because the penguin can't grasp with either its flippers or its webbed feet. It takes food directly with its beak, so it must be able to focus on objects up close. On land, the penguin might be a bit near-sighted because of this feature.

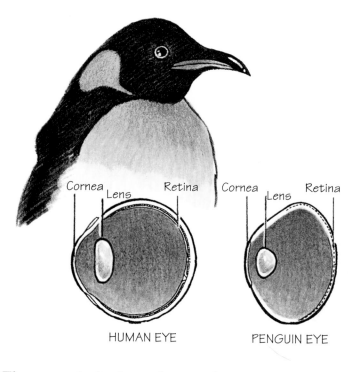

HUMAN EYE

PENGUIN EYE

The penguin is the only vertebrate (animal with a backbone) that has a flat cornea. This feature helps it see well underwater, where it hunts.

Chinstrap penguins, facing page

CATS

(Family: Felidae)

You shine a flashlight under your bed, and two yellow eyes shine back at you . . . . Is it some mysterious creature? Yes—your pet cat! Like many of their wild cat cousins, house cats are nocturnal hunters. Their shining eyes reflect light for better night vision. The reflecting layer in cat eyes is behind the retina. Light that passes through the retina without being absorbed is reflected back again, giving the retina another chance to catch the light. As it passes back out the eye, it creates the spooky shine you see in your cat's eyes.

There are other features of their eyes that strengthen cats' night vision and light-sensitivity. A cat's cornea and lens are both larger and more curved than in the human eye. This makes it possible for a greater number of receptor cells in the retina to be stimulated by light. Cats' retinas also have more layers of light-sensitive rod cells than ours do.

Cats use light 50 percent more efficiently and can see six times better in low light than humans. But their visual acuity is poor. This means that while cats can see more of their surroundings at night than humans can, what they see is out of focus. Why? Because the reflecting layer in the cat's eye blurs the image. The great number of rod cells in the cat's retina also decreases its focusing power. Because their eyes are so sensitive to light, cats' pupils have evolved as vertical slits. These pupils have special muscles that shut out unnecessary light better than round pupils do.

Serval

ANYTHING THAT MOVES

In the wild, large cats like lions, tigers, lynxes, and leopards hunt for their food. So do domestic felines—given half a chance. For this reason, cat eyes have adapted to detect extremely slight movements—such as dinner making a run for it. It's no wonder kittens pounce on anything that moves!

Cats see six times better in low light than humans, but the images they see are blurry.

76

Lion cub, facing page

Hawks

(Order: Falconiformes)

Hawks build nests in the tops of trees, but they hunt from even higher elevations. With vision eight times more powerful than ours, the hawk can spot prey from great height, in great detail. Circling on its powerful wings, the hawk can clearly see the plump field mouse foraging in a field far below; all we would see is a blurry speck—if we could see it at all! Hawk vision is one of the keenest in the animal kingdom. If that field mouse tries to make a run for it, the hawk can follow it, for its eyes can detect slight movement as well as distant objects. Although they look small from the outside, hawk eyes are large in proportion to their bodies, set deep in their head.

Hawks and falcons can be trained to hunt. (A falcon is a hawk with long wings.) When fully trained, these raptors (birds of prey) will leave their perch, hunt their prey, then return to their trainer. This sport is called hawking or falconry. More than 2,500 years ago, the ancient Assyrians caught and trained hawks. And during the Middle Ages, kings and noblemen enjoyed the sport of hawking. After the invention of the shotgun about 400 years ago, men took to hunting with guns instead of birds, and the sport of hawking declined.

INVISIBLE ENEMY

Even a hawk's sharp vision cannot detect the bird's deadliest enemy: poison. Some farmers use poisons called pesticides to protect their crops from pests such as insects and rodents. Birds that eat the poisoned pests become ill, and sometimes sterile as well (unable to produce young). Even hawks that usually live far from human beings are in danger because they stop to feed when they migrate. There, on a peaceful farm, the hawk may meet its invisible foe.

Far up in the sky, a circling hawk spots a plump mouse in the grassy field below. With vision eight times more powerful than human sight, it sees its tiny prey in detail.

Red-tailed hawk, above and facing page

Elephants

(Elephas maximus and *Loxodonta africanus)*

Believe it or not, it's the elephant's trunk that is responsible for the evolution of its eyes. When you look at an elephant from the side, you see just one of its eyes. An elephant has monocular vision, each eye scanning the horizon on its own side. But if you look at an elephant face on, it will look back at you with both eyes pointing forward. This kind of vision is binocular, like yours.

Elephant eyes are adapted for monocular *and* binocular vision. The question is, "why both?" The answer is, "the trunk." If elephants only had monocular vision, they could not focus in front of their faces, where their trunks do their business. Elephants use their trunks (also called a proboscis, from the Greek word for nose) for more than just breathing. They use them to grasp leaves from treetops, to feed themselves, to spray cool water over their backs, and to move objects out of their way. While monocular vision lets an elephant keep an eye on its side surroundings, binocular vision allows the animal to keep track of its trunk.

SIZING THINGS UP

When it comes to eye size, elephants take the prize. No other land mammal has eyes as big as an elephant's. Only whales, which are sea mammals, have eyes that are bigger. Yet, in proportion to the size of the elephant's body, its eyes aren't really all that big. Horses and zebras are ten times smaller than elephants, but their eyes are almost as large.

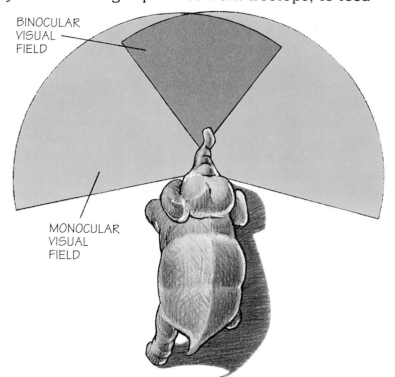

BINOCULAR VISUAL FIELD

MONOCULAR VISUAL FIELD

The monocular visual field is the area each of the elephant's eyes sees on its own. The binocular visual field is the area the eyes see together when they look forward.

African elephant, facing page

ZEBRAS

(Genus: *Equus*)

Zebra eyes are adapted for one main purpose: spotting danger. Set far back and wide-apart on their long faces, zebra eyes have a very wide angle of vision. With a sweep of their head, they can take in a panorama of their native African savanna. Even while grazing, zebras keep watch above the grass tops with their high-set eyes. When a zebra spots a predator, such as a lion, its defense strategy is simply to run—fast!

Located on the sides of the head, each zebra eye has a monocular visual field of 146 degrees (about a third of a circle). When the zebra points its eyes forward, these fields of vision overlap for binocular vision. Working together, the eyes share a binocular field of 65 degrees (less than a quarter of a circle). This is much narrower than the binocular field of carnivores (meat-eaters), who need good depth perception to hunt. Zebras are herbivores (plant-eaters) and feed on grasses.

Like cats, dogs, and other animals, zebra eyes have a reflecting layer that increases the amount of light absorbed by the rods in the retina. Zebras can therefore see extremely well at night. They don't, however, focus as quickly as most animals do. Instead, zebras see long and short distances out of different parts of their eyes. To bring images into sharp focus, zebras use the upper part of their eyes only.

Burchell's zebra

DON'T BE SHY

Zebras and horses are cousins, both members of the genus *Equus*. Have you ever wondered why wagon horses wear blinders, leather flaps that block the animal's side vision? Horses, like zebras, have wide fields of vision, but their eyes focus slowly. The sudden movement of a bird swooping or a car speeding by therefore can startle a horse and cause it to bolt or rear. This is called "shying," and it can be dangerous. If a horse shies on a busy street, for example, it may dart in front of a moving car. Blinders help horses focus calmly on what's ahead.

Even while grazing, zebras keep a lookout over the grass tops for predators, such as leopards.

Grevy's zebra, facing page

AN ANCIENT SENSE

Touch is perhaps the oldest sense there is. Prehistoric creatures may not have been able to see very well in the dark ocean depths, but they could feel. Even now, millions of years later, touch is the first sense humans rely on when we come into the world. When you were a baby, you felt things—such as your crib, your blanket, and your mother's hands—before your eyes could focus or sounds had any meaning. You first discovered your toes not by sight but by touch. You put small objects in your mouth not to taste them but to feel them.

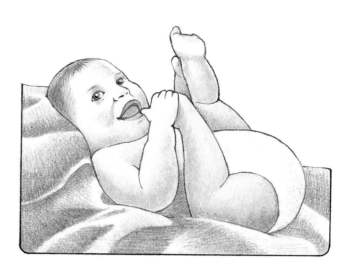

Touch is the first sense we use when we come into the world.

Animals use their sense of touch to locate food, identify members of their family or species, move around safely in their habitat, find mates, and more. The sense of touch also helps animals, including humans, detect danger and avoid injury. Because of our sense of touch, we can experience pleasant sensations, such as stroking a pet's fur or cuddling with those we love. In fact, in many animal species "cuddling" seems to help young animals (including children) become healthy adults. Children who are held and hugged usually grow up to be happier and more confident than those who were not.

What Touch Tells Us

The sense of touch is sometimes divided into other senses because it covers so many types of **tactile sensation** (physical feeling). The human organs for touch, for example, can detect pressure, pain, temperature, movement, and texture, as well as more subtle sensations. We can stand outside and, from the air on our skin, tell whether it's hot, warm, cool, or cold. Some people claim they can detect tiny changes in air pressure and so can "feel" an approaching storm. We run our fingertips across a surface and immediately know if it is smooth or rough, hard or soft, wet or dry, slippery or sticky. A spider creeps up our arm and we jerk reflexively, knowing just where the creature is even though we haven't yet looked. We hold something between our thumb and forefinger and judge how thick or thin it is. We hold a rock in our hand and get a sense of its weight. We hold a feather in the other hand and feel its lightness. We sit on a tack—and yowl in pain! Our sense of touch provides all of these different kinds of information.

Our sense of touch gives us information about our environment and allows us to feel pleasant sensations.

Feelers Galore

Not all touch sense organs are alike—far from it. Mammals' touch organs are most often nerves embedded in their skin. Many insects have touch-sensitive hairs on their antennae and even all over their bodies; these are called sensilla. Believe it or not, cats and walruses have a touch organ in common: the long whiskers on their faces, called vibrissae. Other animals use their sense of touch to detect vibration. This is how the orb web spider catches its prey.

Some parts of an animal's body may be more sensitive to touch than others. The hairs between a cat's paw pads are extremely ticklish, for instance. The mole's pink nose is very sensitive and easily hurt. In humans, the fingertips, lips, nose, cheeks, and mouth are among the most sensitive body parts.

The Purpose of Pain

Aches, pains, pangs, burns, twinges, cramps—it's no fun to feel any of them. But imagine if you could feel no pain. If you grabbed a dish right out of the oven with your bare hands, you wouldn't feel a thing as it burned you. If you pulled a muscle while running, you'd just keep on moving, damaging the muscle even more. You might not even notice if you broke a bone! Fortunately, all of these things normally hurt—and trigger a reflex in you to stop whatever is causing the pain and seek help if necessary. In general, physical pain is a message that your body is under stress or has been injured and needs to heal. The pain generally goes away on its own when health is restored.

Touch Telegraph

Despite all of these different kinds of feelers, there are some common elements to the sense of touch. Cells that receive physical cues such as pressure, warmth, or pain are called **touch receptors**. Touch receptors in humans are bundles of nerves in our skin. These cells convert this information into an electrical signal and send it through the animal's nervous system to the brain. The brain then perceives (understands) the signal as touch and determines what kind of touch it is and what the animal should do in response to it.

This book can only touch on a few of the fascinating things there are to learn about feelers in the animal kingdom. But it will introduce you to many of the interesting ways animals relate to their environment and to each other. We hope this book sparks you to learn more about the sense of touch. If you want to review a term (*touch receptor*, for example), or if you come across a word you don't understand (what's *habitat*?), turn to the glossarized index at the back. But first, let's enter the bizarre and beautiful world of feelers.

We're lucky we can feel pain. Lucky?! Yes. Without it we could seriously injure ourselves and not even know it.

Praying Mantis

(Mantis religiosa)

Mediterranean mantis

One look at the praying mantis and you'll know how the insect got its name. When it moves, this slender, stick-like creature creeps slowly, turning its inquisitive face in an almost human way. More often, the insect perches with its front legs uplifted as though in prayer. These powerful forelegs are actually poised to snap out at unsuspecting insects that wander by. The mantis then turns its prey over and begins munching away, biting into the back of the insect's neck to sever the main nerve.

The praying mantis is an extremely successful hunter, snaring its prey a surprising 85 percent of the time. The primary tool this masterful hunter uses is its sense of touch. As it awaits its prey, the mantis is responding to information coming from hundreds of touch-sensitive hairs called sensilla. These hairs sit in a socket connected to a nerve cell. There are more than 400 hairs in each of the two hair beds on either side of the mantis' neck alone! That's not bad for an insect that measures only one to a few inches long.

The mantis always turns its head to look directly at its prey. The insect knows how far its legs should strike to capture the victim by how far its head has turned. But it has to move very fast and with great accuracy. Its big eyes aren't keen enough for the job. The praying mantis' perfect aim comes from its sense of touch, by way of the tiny hairs on its neck.

PREYING MANTIS

Praying mantises are harmless to humans, but otherwise they are fearsome fighters. The mantis itself seems afraid of nothing. It has even been known to box with kittens and to grab hummingbirds at birdfeeders! The insect's superb balance is also due to its sense of touch. Beds of sensilla located throughout the body and leg joints are stimulated as the mantis moves so it can balance on its rear quarters. From this position, it can accurately attack just about anything that moves.

The praying mantis severs the main nerve of its prey before eating it.

Praying mantis, facing page

Orb Web Spiders

(Family: Araneidae)

If you drop a line and hook into a lake to catch a fish, you won't see, hear, smell or taste the fish until you've reeled it in. You depend entirely on your sense of touch to know when you have a nibble on your line.

Spiders that build orb webs "fish" for insects in a similar way. First, the spider builds its complex web. Amazingly, this takes only about one hour. Next, the spider sits in the center of the web, head down, with its feet lightly touching the sticky lines. Then, an insect flies into the web and becomes stuck. It wriggles, trying to free itself. The web moves. Sensing these vibrations with its feet, the spider knows that dinner may be at hand. It follows the tugs on the lines to locate its victim.

Relying on the sense of touch, rather than vision or hearing, has important advantages. The web spider can hunt on a dark, moonless night as easily as in the daytime. Also, the strength of the vibration tells the spider important information about what type of prey has been caught. If the web vibrates only slightly, the spider knows its victim is small and defenseless. It races quickly to its victim, bites the tiny insect, and drags it back to its feeding area. If the web shakes wildly, the spider approaches cautiously, knowing the insect is large and could be dangerous.

Cobwebs that gather in the corners of rooms and behind furniture are webs left behind by spiders who moved on or died. But most spiders don't just leave their old haunts: they eat them before respinning a new one.

AVOIDING THE TRAP

Did you ever wonder how a spider avoids getting caught in its own trap—the sticky web? It's as easy as one-two-three! First, the spider keeps its body off of the sticky, silken threads. Second, it has special claws at the end of its legs that only lightly touch the web's threads. And third, it secretes a special oil on its legs so the threads of the web won't stick to them.

The orb web spider locates prey by following the vibrations the trapped insect makes when it struggles.

Orb-weaving spider, above and facing page

Grasshoppers

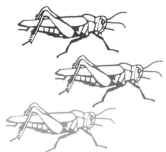

(Family: Acrididae)

Short-horned grasshopper

At small airports you can see a wind sock fluttering in the breeze on top of the control tower. Pilots check the wind sock to see from which direction and how strong the wind is blowing. For a safe take-off, airplanes need to propel down the runway into the wind.

Grasshoppers take off all the time. But they don't use a propeller to get airborne: their large hind legs launch them. For a successful lift-off, they too must propel themselves into the wind. But how does the insect know which way the wind blows? Its sense of touch tells it.

A grasshopper may look like it's covered with green armor, but this crusty shell is actually covered with many fine, touch-sensitive hairs called sensilla. Five different groups of sensilla grow on the grasshopper's head alone. If the air around the hopper's head moves only slightly, the sensilla can detect it. In fact, scientists measured a reaction in a grasshopper when its sensilla was moved less than a millionth of a foot! When the sensilla move, they stimulate nerve cells that send signals to the grasshopper's brain. The brain then determines if the direction and velocity (speed) of the wind are right for take-off.

The types of sensilla on the hopper's body serve different purposes. Some act as an alarm if another creature tries to grab the insect. Some alert the hopper when dirt or debris strikes its body. These sensilla trigger a grooming response.

WHY SO MANY SENSILLA?

Scientists remain puzzled as to why grasshoppers are covered with so many types of touch receptors. There are many sensilla on the hopper's underside. Do these tell the insect to elevate its belly so it won't get stuck to a sticky leaf? There are also sensilla on the inside of the insect's legs; these are called the Brummer's organ. When the hopper is still, this organ rests against the side of its body. Does this have something to do with the instinct to hop? There is a lot we don't understand about grasshoppers.

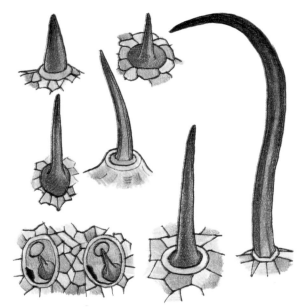

The grasshopper's body is covered with different types of touch-sensitive hairs called sensilla.

Venezuelan grasshopper, facing page

Sand Scorpions

(Order: Scorpionida)

This interesting creature has poor vision. It doesn't smell the insects it feeds on. And it doesn't hear them either. How does it manage to find its prey? Touch-sensitive hairs on its eight legs accurately sense the vibrations insects make when they move in the sand. These hairs are called—you guessed it—sensilla.

Sand scorpions live in the hot, dry Mojave Desert, where temperatures soar to over 150° degrees F (70° C) in the middle of a summer day. Nighttime is the right time for hunting if you're a sand scorpion. In the relative cool of the evening, the scorpion emerges from its underground burrow to perch on the sand. It sits very still, sometimes waiting for several hours for a moth, insect, or even a smaller sand scorpion to wander by. When it hunts, the scorpion relies on the sensilla on its eight legs to detect information about the presence and location of a possible meal. When prey ventures near, the scorpion opens its pedipalps (prey-capturing pincers), extends them forward, and raises its body off the sand. It stays motionless when the prey is still. But each time the insect moves even slightly, the scorpion creeps closer. At last, it snatches its prey! The scorpion then paralyzes it with a poisonous sting from the end of its tail.

Scorpions are arachnids, like their eight-legged cousins the spider, mite, and tick. They can reach a length of 3 inches (about 8 centimeters) and, if undisturbed, live for five or six years. Their stings can be fatal even to large animals and humans. You know what else? Some sand scorpions appear flourescent under ultraviolet light—they glow in the dark.

Parabuthus scorpions

TIME TO LAY LOW

Sometimes a scorpion has bad luck in hunting. If it has been a long time since its last meal, the scorpion can "turn down" its metabolism. (Metabolism is the rate at which an animal uses its energy.) Then it stays inactive inside its burrow and can survive in this semi-dormant state for several weeks or even a few months.

The sensilla on the scorpion's eight legs detect the movement of prey in the sand.

Tail and stinger of African emperor scorpion, facing page

TIGer SWaLLowtAils

(Papilio glaucus)

In the world of butterflies, the tiger swallowtail is a long-distance flier. With its small, lightweight body and large wings, the swallowtail rides the air currents great distances seldom beating its wings. How does it do this? It is very sensitive to changes in air pressure and then to the air currents that these changes create.

The butterfly's nervous system consists of a brain and two nerve cords that run through the body. Small numbers of nerve cells along these cords branch out to all parts of the swallowtail's body. On the butterfly's wings are bristly sensilla (touch-sensitive hairs) that are extremely sensitive to air pressure changes. As the butterfly flies through the air, these bristles tell it where to catch the best gusts of wind on which to glide.

The butterfly's antennae are also amazingly responsive sense organs. They handle the insect's senses of balance and smell. The base of each antenna houses a special organ, called the Johnston's organ, that helps maintain the butterfly's orientation during flight. (Orientation is "getting your bearings," knowing where you are in relation to your surroundings.) Without the Johnston's organ, the butterfly might fly upside down or even in circles!

Butterflies have three pairs of legs, and their sense of touch is important here as well. Sensory cells around the leg joints tell the butterfly how to bend its legs and move its body.

AIRY VEINS

If you look closely at a butterfly's wings, you will see a delicate network of veins. Unlike human veins, which carry life-giving blood, the butterfly's veins contain mainly air. This network of air-filled veins makes the butterfly's wings float like soap bubbles. Over the veins is a layer of colored scales that gives each kind of butterfly its special markings—and that's a lot of markings. There are more than 20,000 species throughout the world. The tiger swallowtail got its name from the yellow or orange and brownish stripes that cover its wings.

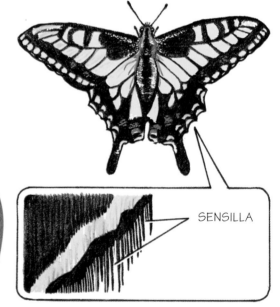

SENSILLA

The tiger swallowtail seldom flaps its wings when it flies. The touch-sensitive bristles on its wings tell the butterfly where to catch gusts of wind on which to glide.

Tiger swallowtail butterfly, above and facing page

TRAP-DOOR SPIDERS

(Family: Ctenizidae)

Trap-door spiders don't weave webs. They live in holes in the ground that they cover with a hinged lid made of spun spider silk. This lid resembles a trap door. When night comes, the trap-door spider pokes its head and front legs out of the opening of its covered burrow. It sits and waits for its next meal to walk or wriggle by.

Any small, passing bug will do. The spider cannot see its prey well in the dark. Crawling bugs do not make much noise. The spider cannot smell them. How does it know that the passing beetle or grasshopper or ant is within reach? The spider's legs, which stretch out from under the trap door, are covered with fine hair. If a passing beetle brushes against these hairs ever so slightly, the spider seizes the unsuspecting insect with its front legs. With its back legs, the spiders anchors itself in its house, and then drags the victim under the trap door.

Another kind of trap-door spider covers its burrow opening with a leaf. When an insect crawls across or lands on the leaf, the leaf vibrates. The spider feels the vibration with its sensitive hairs, which brush against the bottom of the leaf. It then rushes out of the burrow and snares its prey. Still other kinds of trap-door spiders spin "trip wires" of silk in front of their burrows. If an insect stumbles across one, the vibration alerts the spider and it lunges out to attack its prey.

THE NOD OF DEATH

After a trap-door spider drags its prey into its burrow, it raises its head and bites its victim. Why does it give its dinner this little nod? Unlike most spiders, which have fangs that close from each side like pincers, trap-door spiders have jaws similar to ours, with fangs on the top and bottom. When the trap-door spider opens its jaws to bite its victim, it looks like it's nodding its head.

The trap-door spider lies concealed in its burrow. If a passing insect brushes against the fine hairs on its outstretched legs, the spider seizes the unsuspecting animal.

Trap-door spider, above and facing page

Fiddler Crabs

(Uca minax)

Touch is the most important sense to fiddler crabs. It helps them forage for food, detect enemies, find mates, and avoid obstacles. Their amazing tactile ability even helps them maintain their balance. Bristles and hairs are the secret to the crabs' powerful sense of touch. Touch receptor bristles grow all over the crab's body. Most are on the walking legs, especially at the ends.

Hairs on the crab's claws can sense how hard or soft an object is when the crab pinches it. Other specialized hairs, called thread hairs and free hook hairs, allow the crab to detect the direction and strength of water currents as they flow against the crab's body. Other hairs are sensitive to low-frequency vibrations caused by the movement of things nearby. A submerged fiddler crab, for example, will react to a single drop of water falling on the surface over its head.

Despite their name, you won't find fiddler crabs making music. They got their name from their appearance. The male has one very large claw that often is as big as the rest of his entire body. The crab holds this large claw close to his body—and looks like he's playing the fiddle!

Fiddler crabs are small creatures, only about 1 inch (2.5 centimeters) long. They live together in great numbers on tropical sandy beaches. They dig into the sand between the tide lines and come out to feed on microscopic plants and animals when the tide goes out. Females use both claws for feeding. But males can use only their smaller claw. When the tide comes in, all fiddler crabs hide in their individual burrows in the sand.

Fiddler crab claw

WARNING! NO TRESPASSING

Fiddler crabs stridulate. That is, they make a shrill sound like crickets and grasshoppers do. They do this by rubbing a small spike on their elbow against a row of teeth on the edge of their shell. If a crab tries to enter a burrow that's already occupied, the crab inside stridulates. The would-be visitor gets the message and scoots away.

Only male fiddler crabs have one very large claw. The claws of female fiddlers are about the same size.

Male fiddler crab, facing page

GReen Iguanas

(Family: Iguanidae)

The green iguana depends on touch to sense the temperature of the sand it stands on. The animal's survival depends on this ability. Female green iguanas dig burrows in the sand along beaches and lay their eggs in them. They begin by searching for a spot that is just the right temperature. The temperature of the sand must be within 2 degrees of 86° F or the eggs will not hatch. The female lays 20 to 70 eggs that take three months to hatch. Like other lizards, the iguana has touch receptors beneath its toughened, leathery skin. These enable the animal to feel the sand's temperature.

Green iguanas look very awkward with their heavy tails and wide legs. In fact, they are remarkably agile and can scramble easily from one tree to another on connecting branches. All creatures that move about with great agility depend on a highly developed sense of touch. Without the many touch receptors in the skin of their feet, stomach, and tail, the iguana would be clumsy. Imagine how difficult it would be to walk if you couldn't feel the ground with your feet. The iguana could never scurry about if it could not feel where the branches, twigs, and rocks are.

These lizards cannot leap far, but an iguana 50 feet up in a tree will take the short way down: it throws itself to the ground and, without a scratch, quickly scurries off. Iguanas are vegetarians and eat many parts of plants, including flowers, leaves, and fruit. Some young iguanas eat insects. Iguanas are hunted by snakes, human beings, and hawks. In many parts of the world they are considered to be a delicious food.

Front foot of iguana

LIFE AS AN IGUANA

Green iguanas have a combed crest down their backs and are a pale green color. They live in trees in tropical forests and are fond of water. When in danger, the green iguana often will escape to water. They can swim underwater, using their tails to propel them along. They prefer to live in trees overhanging pools or rivers. They come down to the ground only when it's cold to hide beneath logs or in holes.

Its keen sense of touch helps the iguana scurry with ease from tree to tree.

Common iguana, facing page

Mallards

(Anas platyrhynchos)

A duck's bill is hard, like a bone or a shell. Yet it is one of the most sensitive parts of the bird's body. Rows of touch receptors clustered together line the edge of a duck's bill. This feature is especially important to dabbling ducks such as the mallard. Dabblers upend themselves (turn upside down and dive) to forage on the muddy bottom of the lake or river in which they live. They use their sensitive bills to poke around for something good to eat. When ducks dabble, their rear ends stick straight up out of the water. Mallards also feed on the surface of the water and from the mud on the banks.

If a duck is dabbling in water instead of mud, its sensitive tongue gets in on the action. It acts like a straw to suck water into the duck's mouth and then push it out, leaving only edible particles behind. Filters along the edges of the bill let out objects the duck is not interested in eating. Mallards can feed either during the day or night since they don't need sight to forage. They eat leaves, seeds, grains, berries, insects, and small fish.

A duck's webbed feet are also highly sensitive to touch. They may waddle awkwardly, but ducks actually pick their way carefully through sticks and pebbles on the shore or bank. They step on round, smooth objects and steer clear of sharp sticks and rocks. The duck is using its sense of touch to keep its balance and to avoid hurting its feet.

P.S. The wild mallard is the ancestor of most domesticated duck breeds.

FEATHER FEELERS

There are touch receptor cells in the mallard's feathers, in both their long contour feathers and in their short bristling feathers. The receptors in the bristle feathers send messages to the duck's brain about the location of the contour feathers. These cells help the duck arrange its feathers, clean them, and position them properly when flying.

Mallards use their sensitive bills to search for food in the muddy bottoms of lakes and rivers.

Mallard drake (male), above and facing page

SLOThS

(Genus: *Bradypus*)

Tree sloths move very, very slowly. They spend much of their day asleep, hanging upside-down from tree limbs or rolled into a snug ball in the fork of a branch. Once a week or so, they crawl to the ground and amble over to another tree. At night they feed, using their mighty claws to grope around for their favorite foods—tender leaves, twigs, and buds. Their sense of touch helps them find both food and the best passages through the treetops. Their hearing and sight are poor.

Sloths can turn their necks and forearms all the way around to three-quarters of a complete circle. Their front limbs are much stronger and more flexible than the hind ones. The animal can roll its body into a perfect ball, so that its nose touches the top of its tail. Most sloths have a curve in their lower back, just enough to make up for the difference in length between their hind and front legs.

Two-toed sloth? Three-toed sloth? Neither species can move its digits (fingers or toes) independently. They are fused together. If the animal wishes to move to another place in the tree, it uses a slow hand-over-hand motion. Even when perched snugly in the fork of a tree, the sloth's claws are securely hooked to a branch. What if they must defend themselves? Tree sloths can slash quickly and inflict deep wounds. They can also use their teeth in defense. Generally, when left alone, they are gentle creatures. But they are no match for the chainsaw. Sloths are endangered by loss of habitat (living space) because the South American forests in which they live are being cut down.

Three-toed sloth

GREEN HAIR

Imagine moving so slowly that things started to grow on you. Such is the case with the tree sloth. Green algae often grow on these arboreal (tree-dwelling) animals during the wet seasons. These tiny plants live close to the surface of the sloth's crisp, straw-like hairs and give a green tint to its grayish-brown fur.

The sloth spends most of its time hanging upside-down in trees. When it gets hungry, it gropes for tender leaves and buds with its powerful, sensitive claws.

Three-toed sloth's claw, facing page

MORAY EELs

(Family: Muraenidae)

There are 100 species of morays that range in length from 6 inches to 10 feet. If you came eye to eye with a moray of any size, you'd probably get quite a scare! They have sharp fang-like teeth set in a forceful jaw, thick skin without scales, and a body that looks like a snake's. In fact, they are usually very shy and dart back into their holes when large creatures pass by. They have been known to attack, however, when they are cornered or taunted.

The eel is perfectly adapted to life in a reef. Since their heads are shaped like wedges and their bodies are smooth and muscular, they can easily squeeze in and out of nooks and crannies in the rocks. Eels have every reason to stay close to home in both reef and rock. It is here that they can best find the crustaceans and small fish that make up the bulk of their diet. And when eels are not out hunting, crevices make an excellent place to hide from predators.

An unusual reflex helps the eel navigate and hide itself in these tight spaces. This reflex prompts the eel to automatically reorient its body whenever it brushes against a wall of rock or coral. If its tail dangles outside of a crevice, for example, the eel reflexively pulls back inside for protection. This reflex is also found in other reef inhabitants, such as fish that lurk in rock cracks. Special sensory pits that look like dots decorate the faces of some moray eels. These pits sense vibrations in the water and help the eel detect creatures moving nearby.

THE FRIENDLY EEL

Can you imagine petting a moray eel? They may not be the cuddliest of creatures, but some divers have made friends with them. If a moray gets to know a diver who feeds it a fish now and then, the moray may behave like a tame animal. Some will even sit in a diver's hands. But if the diver moves too quickly or jerks the food away, the alarmed moray may bite the hand that feeds it.

The moray eel's keen sense of touch helps it navigate through narrow passages in its reef habitat.

Spotted moray eels, facing page

CATS

(Family: Felidae)

Domestic cat

Cats purr when they're petted and rub up against you when you stop, as if asking for more. Cats like to be touched because it feels good to them. How does a cat feel through the fur covering its body? Many of the strands of hair on a cat's body are rooted directly into sensitive touch receptor cells. When the cat's hair is touched, these receptors alert the cat's brain, which interprets the touch. Some hairs on a cat have a high number and variety of touch receptors. They are sensitive to even the slightest breeze. Other cat hairs require brisk brushing before the cat notices.

The next time you see a cat stalking a mouse, a bird, or a grasshopper, pay special attention to its whiskers. When a cat springs at its prey, its whiskers shoot forward as far as possible. Once the prey is captured, the whiskers curve around the prey to keep track of its movements. A cat's whiskers are densely packed with touch receptors. Even before they are touched, the whiskers can detect the vibrations of nearby movement. Cats also use their whiskers to navigate in the dark. Feeling with its whiskers, a cat easily pads about in a pitch black room, avoiding collisions with walls and objects. Cats' whiskers can also keep them out of too-tight spots. If its whiskers don't easily clear the entrance to an enclosure or passage, the cat will stay out of it.

P.S. The technical term for cat whiskers is vibrissae.

TICKLISH KITTY

Have you ever lightly tickled the hair between a cat's paw pads? The cat will twitch its leg and finally lift its head, hoping you'll leave it alone. A cat's paw pads and the hairs between them are very sensitive to touch. The area on its front legs above the cat's wrist is also thick with a patch of very sensitive hairs. These hairs act like the whiskers, sensing objects not yet touched but close to the paws.

Cats curve their whiskers around captured prey to keep track of its movements.

108

Siberian tiger, facing page

Moles

(Genus: *Scaptonyx*)

Moles spend most of their lives digging in underground tunnels in search of food. They need to eat almost constantly and, in fact, may die if they go without food for even 12 hours. Their favorites are worms and underground insects. Working both day and night, they forage tirelessly for these creatures in their dark world. Moles have tiny, weak eyes, and some are completely blind.

The mole's sense of touch, however, is very keen. The animal's hairless pink snout is covered with thousands of tiny touch sensors called Eimer's organs. Special sensory hairs called vibrissae cover the mole's skin. The mole becomes very alert when its vibrissae detect vibrations. The direction, strength, speed, and duration of these vibrations tell the animal whether there is an insect nearby—food—or possible danger. Working together, the Eimer's organs and vibrissae give the mole an incredibly powerful sense of touch.

Most moles have short tails that are covered with sensory hairs. The mole often holds its tail up so it brushes against the walls and roof of the tunnel. The tail can sense vibrations passing through the soil. But the tail can be more than just a warning system. The star-nosed mole of North America stores fat in its long tail for extra energy during mating season.

Moles are pests to gardeners because they're champion diggers. But there's a sure-fire way to repel them. Push empty bottles into the mole burrows with the necks sticking out of the ground. When the wind blows, it makes a hollow, piping sound in the bottles. The vibrations from this noise will travel into the mole's burrow and drive these super-sensitive creatures away.

Mole paw

VELVETY SOFT

Most moles have very soft fur. The hairs are all about the same length and will lie in any direction, like velvet. The features of its fur allow the mole to go backwards and forwards with ease in tight burrows. In contrast, many other mammals dislike having their fur rubbed "the wrong way." Stroke a cat from its tail up to its head, for instance, and it will probably flick its tail in annoyance or even stalk away.

The mole's tail brushes against the walls and roof of the burrow to sense vibrations.

Common mole, facing page

Crocodiles

(Genus: *Crocodylus*)

The crocodile's thick, scaly skin is like armor. But despite their hard, bumpy skin, crocodiles are sensitive to touch and seem to enjoy being touched by other crocodiles. Touch receptors are clustered beneath their scales. There are heavy concentrations of these receptors around their heads and necks, so these parts of a crocodile are especially sensitive to touch. Crocodiles often rub snouts and necks with each other, especially before mating. It may be their way of shaking hands, hugging, or just checking each other out.

Crocodiles are reptiles, and reptiles are cold-blooded, which means they can't maintain a constant body temperature like we do. They can't shiver to stay warm or sweat to cool down. But they are still sensitive to hot and cold temperatures, and they like to stay comfortable. When they're cold, they bask in the sun. They retreat to the shade when they're warm. At night, they sleep in the water because it holds heat longer than air does.

When a crocodile is in the water it lays low, only poking its eyes and bulging nostrils above the surface. To hold this position, crocodiles carry several pounds of rocks in their stomach to weigh them down. Otherwise, the natural buoyancy of their lungs would make them float on the surface. In this position, a crocodile can fool other creatures: its thick, bumpy skin looks like an innocent log floating in the water.

American crocodile

CROCODILE TEARS

Crocodiles live in warm rivers and wetlands in Africa, Asia, Australia, and America. Most crocodiles eat a variety of food, including insects, spiders, frogs, fish, snakes, small mammals, and smaller crocodiles. Very large crocodiles—some reach a length of more than 20 feet (7 meters)—also eat large mammals and have been known to attack humans. More than half of the 21 species of crocodiles are endangered because humans hunt them to make shoes, belts, and purses out of their skin.

Crocodiles have many touch receptors around their heads and necks. They often rub necks and snouts with each other.

Crocodile skin, facing page

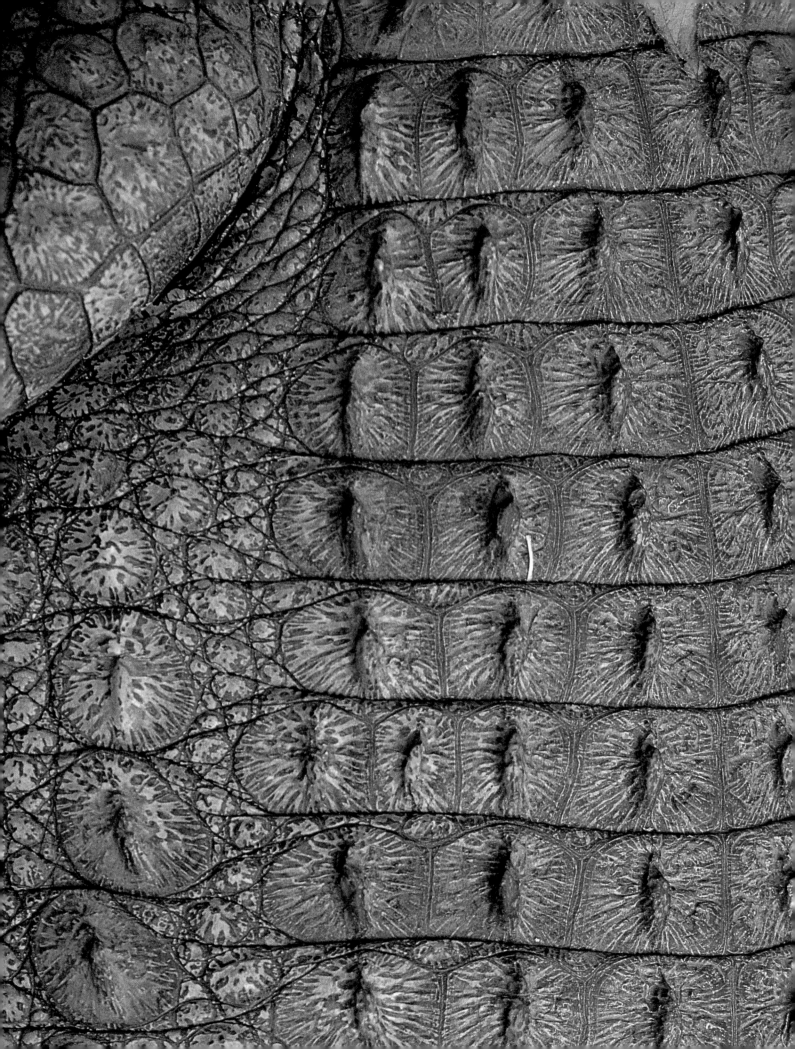

Platypuses

(*Ornithorhynchus anatinus*)

The platypus lives in Australia and is a most unusual animal. It feeds in freshwater, but it is not a fish. It has a bill like a duck, webbed feet, and lays eggs, but it is not a bird of any kind. It spends time both on land and in water, but it is not an amphibian. No, the platypus is a mammal, one of only three known mammals in the world that lays eggs. Once the young are hatched, the platypus suckles them with milk, just like mammals who give birth.

In the evening, the platypus searches for food at the bottom of its lake or pond. When it dives, it plugs its nose and holds its breath—for up to a minute—and closes its eyes and ears to protect them from the muddy water. So how does the platypus find its food? It stirs up the rocky bottom with its bill in search of things that wriggle and squirm, such as worms, larvae, or shrimp.

If you were to reach your hand into the mud at the bottom of a pond, the 20,000 or so touch sensors in your skin would tell you when your fingers touched a rock or a worm. But the platypus' bill, sometimes called its snout, has almost fifty times more touch sensors than your hand does—nearly a million! Some of these sensors on the platypus' bill measure temperature. Others detect texture and movement.

A FEEL FOR LAND AND SEA

Take a close look at the feet of the platypus. They have claws like many other mammals but also webs between them like a duck. These feet are built for life both in water and on land. In the water, the platypus spreads its claws and the webs serve as flippers. On land, the platypus pulls its toes together and its claws stick out to give it a firm grip on the slippery mud. The platypus also uses its claws for digging a burrow, the hole in the ground where it lives and lays its eggs.

The platypus scoops up mud at the bottom of the river with its bill to find worms, larvae, and shrimp.

Platypus, above and facing page

114

GECKOS

(Family: Gekkonidae)

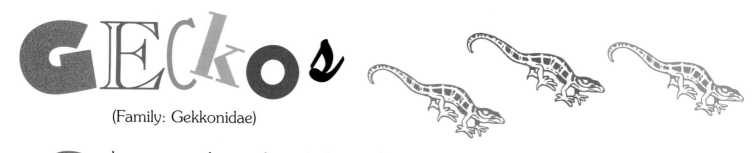

Tokay gecko toes

Geckos can crawl up a glass window and even scurry across a ceiling without falling to the floor. Their amazing feet allow them to grab and hang on to just about any surface. Our hands are very sensitive, but a pane of glass feels completely smooth to us. While we can feel the bumps and ridges in the texture of a wall, we couldn't climb it without a rope or a ladder. What gives geckos such a powerful foothold? It used to be thought that geckos had suction cups on the bottom of their broad flat toes, or that the bottom of their feet were covered with a very sticky substance. Actually, their strange-looking feet are covered with thousands of hooks so small they can only be seen with a microscope. To run across the glass in a window, the gecko finds tiny footholds in the surface of the glass that we cannot feel or even see. With lightning speed, the lizard slips its tiny hooks into these minuscule holes and ridges. Then it reaches forward with another foot, hooks onto more holes and ridges, and releases its grasp on the previous ones. The hooks on a single toe can support many times the weight of an average gecko. The ability to climb on just about any surface allows geckos to catch insects from the underside of tree limbs or in the high corners in houses.

LONG-LIVED LIZARD

Geckos have been around for a long, long time. In fact, they are one of the most ancient animals on Earth. These nocturnal lizards live in warm climates. (Nocturnal means active at night.) They are beneficial to humans because they eat insects that bother us or can even harm us: mosquitoes, flies, ants, and many others. Some geckos live in houses and eat the insects that gather around electric lights. Geckos have large prominent eyes that help them see at night. They have no eyelids and instead moisten their eyes by licking them with their long tongues.

Geckos can scurry across a ceiling without falling to the floor because the bottom of their feet are covered by many tiny hooks that grab the surface.

Tokay gecko, facing page

116

WALRUSES

(Genus: *Odobenus*)

If you're a walrus, every meal is at the bottom of the sea. These animals dive to the ocean floor for food, often staying underwater for up to 10 minutes at a time. Then they swim back to the surface for air. Even though they spend a lot of time in the water, walruses are mammals and so need air to survive.

Almost all of their prey live on or even beneath the sediment that covers the ocean floor. They sense their prey by touch, using their tusks (which are like huge, curved teeth) and their vibrissae. Vibrissae? Yes. Vibrissae are the large facial hairs on the walrus' snout and above its eyes that look like whiskers. But they are more than just whiskers. The walrus uses its vibrissae to dig through the sediment to find its food. The vibrissae grow longer and thicker as the walrus ages.

The walrus eats mostly mollusks, small shellfish. But they don't eat the shell. They suck the animal out of its home and leave the shell behind. They can eat thousands of mollusks in a single day.

Sometimes food is scarce, and walruses must try even harder to probe for their next meal. Scientists have found furrows and shallow pits in the sea bottom where walruses went "rooting" for prey. That can leave a lasting impression on the ocean bottom.

These animals are white or light gray in color. They almost always travel in small groups. Sometimes they gather together in herds of up to several thousand.

ICE IS NICE

Walruses live mostly on floating ice over shallow waters of the North American continental shelf. They prefer ice for resting, mating, and bearing young. If no ice is handy, they'll go to the land—usually small, rocky islands. They lounge close together, often with the youngsters lying on top of the adults. The baby calf stays with its mother at least two years, sometimes longer if no younger sibling is born.

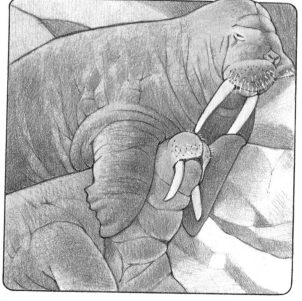

Walruses live together in large herds on floating ice. They lie close to one another.

Walrus, facing page

118

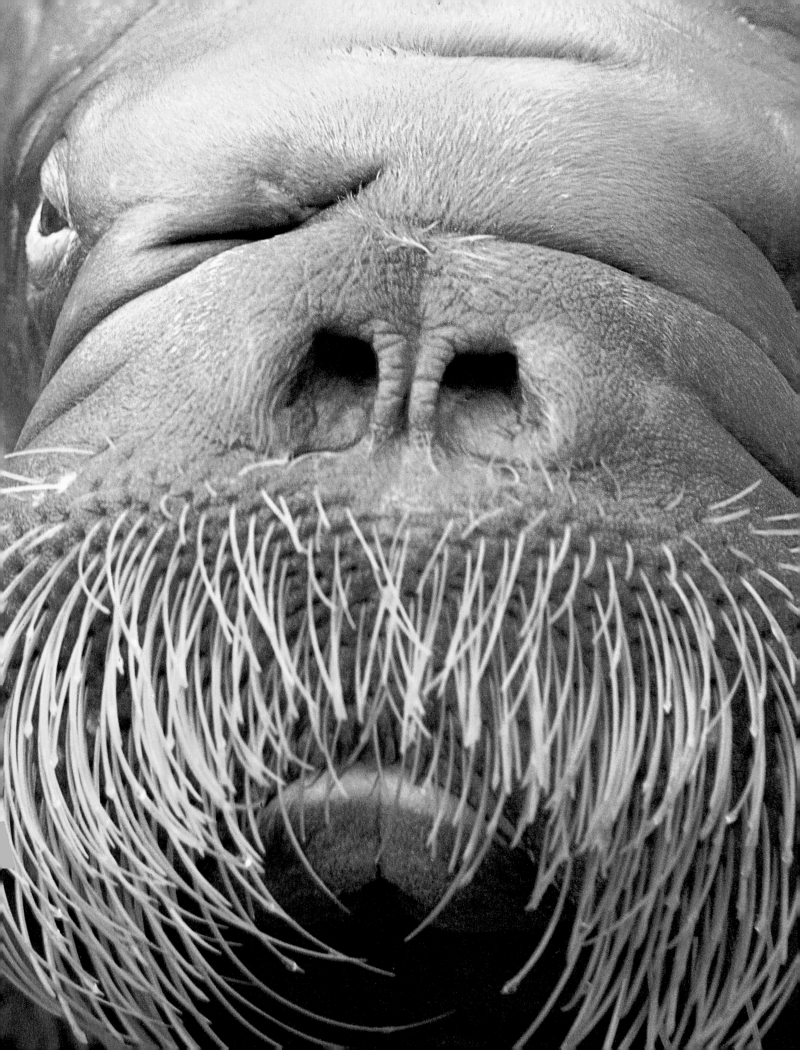

ORANGUTANS

Pongo pygmaeus

(Genus: *Pongo*)

Orangutans, like humans, are primates. They have long arms and strong, hook-shaped hands and feet. They climb or swing between trees in the tropical forests with great ease, aided by their big grasping thumbs. They never let go of one branch until they have a solid grip on another. These large apes have a high number of touch receptors in the skin of their hands and feet. Much of the orangutan's brain is devoted to processing information from these touch receptors.

Orangutans need to eat a lot of food. Sometimes they will munch steadily for an entire day. Fruit makes up more than half of their entire diet. They especially love mangoes, figs, jackfruit, and durians. Their sensitive hands are very useful in gathering fruit because they often explore parts of trees that are hidden from sight. They use only their fingers, not their whole hand, to squeeze fruit to see if it's ripe, just like humans do. Orangutans also eat tender leaves, insects, bark, eggs, and squirrels. They drink water from tree holes, using their hands to gather the water. They slurp the liquid as it dribbles down their hairy wrists.

Orangutans also have touch receptors in strands of their hair. But the soles of their feet and the palms of their hands are the most sensitive areas, and the most useful to them.

RED-HEADED ISLANDERS

Orangutans are large, red-haired apes that live in the jungles of Borneo and Sumatra, Southeast Asian islands. Adult males are about 4.5 feet (1.4 meters) tall and weigh 150 pounds (68 kilograms). They are arboreal (tree-dwelling) creatures and rarely spend time on the ground. They eat an enormous amount of food, mostly fruit, and their sensitive touch enables them to select ripe fruit from high branches out of their view. They are mostly solitary creatures and live long lives. Because of increased logging in their forests, the range of their habitat has decreased substantially in recent years.

Orangutans grope with their sensitive hands for food they can't see.

Adult male orangutan, facing page

LED BY THE NOSE

The sense of smell is especially important in detecting danger, even for humans. We can smell a fire, for example, even when we cannot see or hear it. The advance warning gives us a better chance of escaping the danger. Our sense of smell also unlocks the world of pleasant fragrances—our favorite foods cooking, the outdoors, flowers in bloom, or the salty spray of the ocean. And if we couldn't smell, much of our food would be tasteless to us.

Our sense of smell can warn us of danger. It also allows us to enjoy pleasant fragrances.

Different animals tune in to different odors and ignore or avoid others. For example, a cat will probably turn its nose up at your vegetable garden, but a rabbit will show great interest in the fragrance of carrots and lettuce. This is because animals pay attention to the smells that are important to their survival. Humans can identify thousands of odors, but smell is not one of our most important senses.

What Smells?

Daisies smell fresh, pineapples smell fruity, attics smell musty, and dogs . . . just plain smell! But no matter how we might describe them, all odors are tiny particles of chemical substances that are carried through air, water, or earth and are detected by animals' smelling organs.

Most species of animals have a distinct odor. For example, even with your eyes closed and your ears plugged, you could still probably tell the difference between a parrot and a horse by the way each smells. Animals smell a certain way because of what they eat, where they live, and the natural scents they produce. Many animals have scent glands that secrete a substance that other members of their species can detect. This chemical substance is called a **pheromone** (FAIR-uh-moan). Humans as a species also have a distinct scent (just ask any deer during hunting season). Each individual person, too, has a unique smell. This scent is most likely pleasant to the people who care about us and may be unpleasant to people who dislike us. Think about it: Do you tend to like the smell of people you care about? Do you associate certain smells with certain feelings, activities, or people? It's no surprise if you do: in most people, smells trigger memories more than any other sense.

Smells trigger memories more than any other sense.

Olfactory Organs

Not all smelling organs are conventional noses, snouts, or beaks. The elephant's long trunk, for example, is a multipurpose organ the animal uses to breathe, smell, spray water, feed itself, move obstacles out of the way, and even hug its children. The snake has two openings in the roof of the mouth called the Jacobson's organ with which it smells. A mosquito's smelling organs are on its antennae, as are the

SAVORY SMELLS

When you have a cold and your nose is stuffy, you can't smell a thing. And no wonder: your nasal passages are swollen from inflammation (painful irritation of tissue). This swelling prevents scent molecules from reaching the olfactory receptors far up in your nasal cavities. You may also have noticed that foods you normally love taste bland and boring when you're stuffed up. This is because the sense of smell is all wrapped up with the sense of taste. Flavors are detected by the taste buds covering our tongues, but our perception of them is strengthened by the odors that tag along. These odors travel to the olfactory receptors through your throat as well as through your nose. This is why professional wine tasters swirl the glass of wine under their nose before taking a sip. They are releasing scent molecules from the liquid so they can "taste" the smell of the wine as well as its flavor. Next time you have a cold, close your eyes and put a slice of apple on your tongue and then a slice of raw potato. Can you tell the difference between them?

bee's and moth's. And some species of salamander breathe and smell right through their skin!

Sensing Scents

But whatever the type of organ, all smell is possible because of cells called **olfactory receptors**. Throughout the animal kingdom, these are simple nerve cells with hair-like projections to receive scent molecules. Some animals have greater numbers of olfactory receptors than others, and the receptors are not on the same part of each animal's body. But the way in which the receptors are activated and pass their information on to the brain is the same across species.

The chemical particles that make up odors must first be dissolved before they can be smelled. When the chemicals reach the olfactory receptors, they are turned into signals to be sent to the **olfactory lobe**, the part of the brain that interprets smell. The brain determines what the smell is and then tells the animal what action to take, if any.

This book can only give you a whiff of all the fascinating things there are to learn about noses and the sense of smell. But it will introduce you to many of the interesting ways animals relate to their environment and to each other. We hope this book sparks you to learn more about the sense of smell. If you want to review a term (*olfactory lobe*, for example), or if you come across a word you don't understand (what does *sensilla* mean?), turn to the glossarized index at the back. But first, let's enter the bizarre and beautiful world of noses.

The sense of smell is directly linked to the sense of taste. That's why food tastes bland when you have a cold.

123

Mosquitoes

(Genus: *Culex*)

Mosquitoes don't have noses like ours, but they can still smell. The very fine sensory hairs on their long antennae detect both odors and temperature. Have you ever wondered why mosquitoes seem especially fond of buzzing around your head? It's because you, like all mammals, exhale carbon dioxide. The mosquito's antennae search for carbon dioxide and changes in air temperature because both are clues that a warm-blooded animal is nearby—and that means a meal. Both male and female mosquitoes drink nectar from flowers, but only female mosquitoes drink blood. This is because most types of mosquitoes need a blood meal to develop their eggs.

Mosquitoes are among the most dangerous insects to human beings because many species carry serious diseases. That's why people have invented ways to repel mosquitoes, such as window screens, net drapes over beds, and chemical sprays. If a mosquito flying toward a meal smells something unpleasant, such as a chemical repellent, it changes course and heads in the other direction. Fortunately, you don't have to drench yourself with repellent to keep mosquitoes from pestering you. Usually, it's enough to cover your socks or some other part of your clothing, or even the floor of a porch. Mosquitoes are bothered by the smell of the repellent in the air, not on your skin.

Mosquitoes also use their sense of smell to find a place to nest. They need to lay their eggs in very still ponds or puddles. The insects are attracted to stagnant water by the sweet smell of bacteria that grow in it.

REPEL THE NATURAL WAY

Some unfortunate people are very attractive to mosquitoes. Others, for some mysterious reason, are never bothered by them. Scientists suspect the difference has something to do with the chemicals in human sweat. Fortunately, there are other natural odors that turn mosquitoes off: pennyroyal, eucalyptus, citronella, lavender, and cinnamon are some of them. Some campers rub these oils on their clothing to ward off the pests.

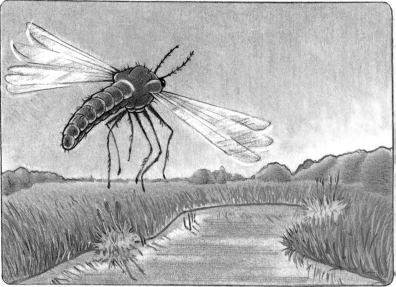

Mosquitoes lay hundreds of eggs in still pools of water. They are drawn to stagnant water by the smell of bacteria.

Mosquito, above and facing page

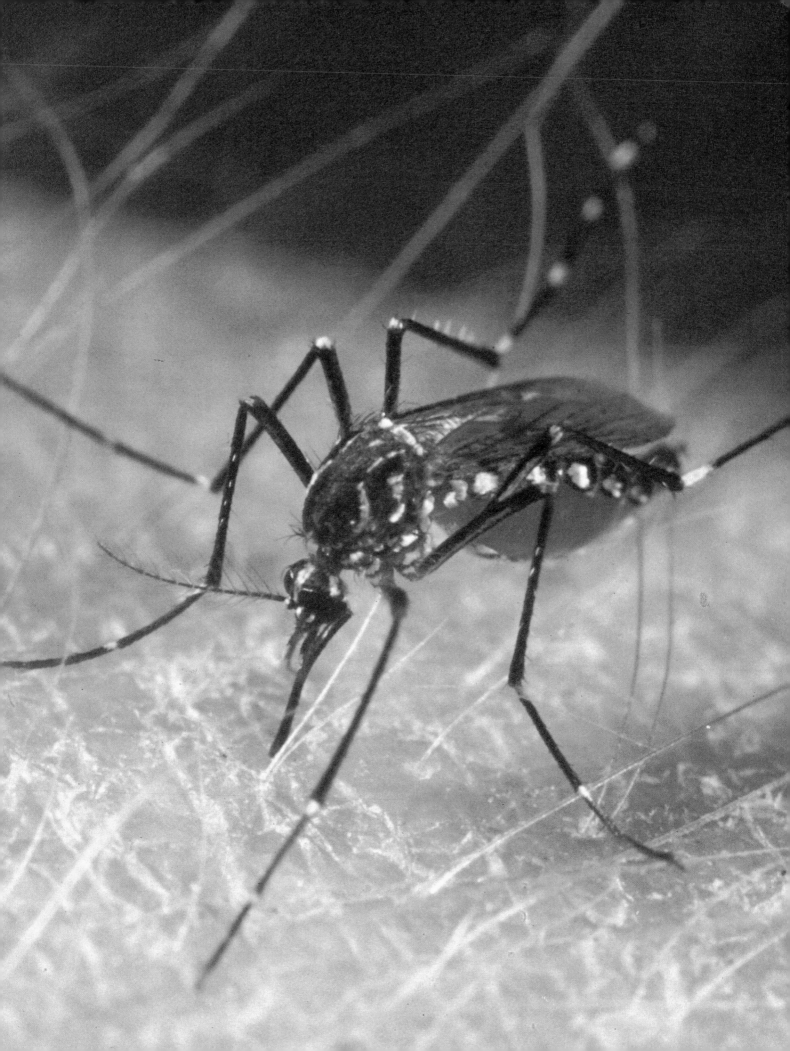

MOThs

(Order: Lepidoptera)

Moths never grow old—they live only a couple of days! Their main purpose in the balance of nature is to serve as food for other, larger animals such as bats and birds. The most important activity for a moth during its brief life is to find a mate quickly and reproduce more moths. The male moth's nose plays a key role in this.

When the female moth emerges from her cocoon, she is odorless because she is not yet prepared to mate. But in just a few hours, she matures, ready to get down to the business of making more moths. At that time, she releases a fine mist of special perfume from two small pouches at the end of her abdomen. This perfume is very attractive to male moths. When just a few tiny molecules of the scent reach the male's antennae, he uses all of his energy to find the female. The female moth can attract males from as far away as three miles. During one scientific experiment, a male moth took just ten minutes to reach a scenting female one mile away. That's faster than a person can walk! Fortunately for male moths, most of them don't have to travel so far to find a mate.

The male moth's antennae, which look like tiny feathers or palm fronds, are much fancier than the female's. There are more than 40,000 sensory nerve cells on these feathery combs. With all of this smelling power, you'd think male moths would be bombarded by odors all the time. But the male moth's "nose" knows only one thing: the scent of the female's perfume.

Elephant hawk moth

A LITTLE DAB'LL DO

The female moth's perfume is incredibly strong. Only .01 microgram (a millionth of a gram) can, in theory, excite a billion or more males. And just how heavy is a gram? About the weight of a female moth.

There are tens of thousands of sensory nerve cells on the male moth's feathery antennae.

Clouded yellow moth, facing page

Ants

(Family: Formicidae)

What does an ant do if it finds a dead butterfly too heavy to carry back to the nest? It heads for home—lickety split—to get help. It pushes its stinger out of its abdomen and drags it along the ground as it crawls. At the same time, it presses on a scent gland that secretes a special chemical called a pheromone. By depositing traces of its pheromone, the ant makes a "sniffable" map for the members' colony to follow back to the prey.

An ant's scent map lasts only a couple of minutes, but other ants replenish the pheromone as they crawl along the same trail. Once the ants haul the food back to the nest, the scent trail vanishes—no more food, no more scent. Ants use scent and smell for other reasons, too. If an intruder disturbs the ants' nest, those ants first to notice emit a pheromone that says "Help! We're being attacked!" That's why if you disturb an ant hill, hundreds of ants will suddenly pour out of the holes and begin swarming around. If they're the kind that bite, you'd better scram!

Ants also secrete other pheromones to attract mates, to establish the order of dominance within the colony, and to identify members of the same colony. So while humans communicate with each other (mainly) through speech and gestures, ants "talk" by giving off scents and "listen" by smelling them.

Bulldog ant

SMELL? WHAT SMELL?

Each of the many ant species has its own unique set of pheromone scents that are top secret and not recognized by other species. For example, if a red ant crosses the pheromone trail a fire ant made, the red ant won't even notice! Its scent detectors are tuned in only to the pheromones of its own species.

Ants leave a trail of scent to lead other ants to a food source. In reality, this trail is invisible.

Ponerine ant, facing page

Bees

(Order: Hymenoptera)

Ouch! That hurts! When a bee stings you it discharges venom (poison) and an odor that may smell somewhat like a banana. This smell is a pheromone that serves as an alarm to other bees. If you are near the hive, the scent may provoke an angry mob of worker bees to swarm over you and sting you repeatedly. That's why most beekeepers are careful to wear protective clothing.

When a worker bee finds a new source of pollen, it releases a pheromone. As the scent of the pheromone wafts through the air, it attracts other worker bees. Soon, they show up at the flower to help collect the pollen.

How do bees detect these pheromones? Their antennae are covered with thousands of sense organs known as sensilla. Among them are tiny pits that contain olfactory (smelling) organs. Some of these olfactory pits react to many different odors, some only to special smells. The queen bee has up to 2,400 olfactory pits. Workers have about 1,600. The drones can have a whopping 37,800!

When a bee returns to the hive laden with nectar for making honey or with pollen to eat, it also carries the smell of the flower that produced the nectar or pollen. The worker bees in the hive use their sensilla to examine the smell clinging to the bee. Then, they set out to find the source of the nectar or the pollen by following traces of its smell in the air. They're helped in their search by a tail-wagging dance the returning bee performs for them—a "bee sign language" that shows the way to the source.

Honeybee

ONE BIG HAPPY FAMILY

Bees live together by the thousands in groups called colonies. A bee's home is called a hive. The bees who gather nectar to make honey are the female workers. Their stingless brothers are called drones. The mother of them all is called the queen.

A worker bee returns to its hive laden with pollen, leaving a scent trail for other workers to follow back to the source of the pollen.

Golden northern bumblebee, facing page

Turtles

(Order: Chelonia)

Turtles have been around a very long time. Fossils have been found of turtles that lived over 200 million years ago! Compare that with the amount of time humans in our current form have been around—only 40,000 years or so. But despite their lengthy stay on earth, turtles today are very similar to their prehistoric ancestors.

Turtles are toothless reptiles closely related to snakes and lizards. Most reptiles have well-developed nasal cavities (a space behind each nostril where the olfactory organs are), but turtles do not. Most reptiles evolved to depend a great deal on their sense of smell. But turtles appear to have survived over millions of years without even developing a sensitive nose! There is at least one exception, however. Snapping turtles apparently can find food in lakes even when the water is too dirty to see through. Scientists believe they do so by smelling their prey. The musk turtle has a gland that emits a very strong, unpleasant smell. This smell is so potent some people call these turtles "stinkpots." The smell may be an alarm that warns other turtles of danger. Or it may serve to attract a mate—after all, the turtles don't seem to mind the smell! It may even be the way musk turtles communicate with other musk turtles. Scientists don't know for certain.

Galapagos tortoise

TURTLE TROUBLE

Even though turtles are among the oldest species on the planet, many types are endangered. In some countries, people eat turtles. The green turtle is almost extinct because it has been hunted for its meat. Other people kill tortoises for their shells. Some rare species are dying out because their habitats (where they live) are destroyed by pollution or development. Some people are trying to save rare and endangered turtles by raising them in captivity or by preserving their natural habitats.

Unlike other reptiles, most turtles do not have a well-developed sense of smell.

Eastern box turtle, facing page

132

FROGs

(Order: Salientia)

There are over 2,000 species of frogs and toads. Toads look very similar to frogs but have rougher, drier skin and tend to spend more time on land than water-loving frogs. These amphibians (animals that live both in water and on land) live on every continent except the frozen land of Antarctica.

And just how well do frogs smell? From species to species, the frog's smelling ability differs a great deal. The leopard frog, for example, can be taught to distinguish between different smells. In one experiment, a frog was reluctant to eat food that had been dipped in rosewater, which has a strong floral smell. Frogs can also find their way back to their home pond—even frogs that are deaf and blind. They accomplish this primarily by using their sense of smell. However, the ability to orient themselves is also strong in frogs. (To orient yourself means to locate yourself in relation to something else—your home, for example.) If frogs are prevented from using their sense of smell (in scientific experiments, for example), they can still find their way home. You have many ways to orient yourself. Your home, your neighborhood, your school, your favorite park or playground— these are all landmarks to help you find your direction. The frog also uses many senses and signals to remember where it lives.

THE SMELL IS THE BELL

Tadpoles of certain amphibians swim around like an orderly school of small fish. They actually swim in rows. But if even a tiny amount of an "alarm" substance enters the water, order breaks down completely. The tadpoles head in every direction. Most swim towards the safety of deeper water. But if their sense of smell is blocked, tadpoles will continue to swim along as if nothing happened. The alarm bell is the smell!

Tadpoles normally swim in orderly rows. If a smell that threatens them enters the water, they will scatter in all directions.

North American tree frog, facing page

Gerbils

(Genus: *Gerbillus*)

Just as ants, bees, and other insects communicate by smell, so does the Mongolian gerbil. This small rodent lives in eastern Mongolia, Northwest China, and western Manchuria. Today, it is also a common pet in America. It spends a great deal of its time rubbing its belly, chin, and neck over small objects.

Why does the gerbil behave in this interesting manner? To communicate with other gerbils. The gerbil has scent glands in the middle of its abdomen and on its chin and neck that secrete pheromones. To leave a mark or a trail of scent, the gerbil rubs its glands on twigs, stones, grass, or other objects in its small world. Scientists aren't completely sure what purpose the scent markings serve, but other gerbils are certainly interested in them. They can tell subtle differences in the odors of the scent trails and can identify where another gerbil has passed by.

There is an amazing feature of their fur that helps gerbils leave their scent trails. The hairs that cover the area near the scent glands have little grooves in them. This helps to move the scent along, as if it were being rolled down a tiny chute or pulled along with a straw.

ATTRACTION BY AROMA

All mammals produce scent, and some of it is used to attract a mate. We don't usually think of ourselves as having this in common with other animals, but consider the rituals we go through when we want to impress someone: we use minty toothpaste, splash on aftershave or dab on perfume, style our hair with mousse or gel, rub fragrant lotion on our skin, and wear freshly laundered clothes. All these things smell good and—we hope—make us attractive.

To leave a scent mark, the gerbil rubs a twig over the scent gland on its chin. Gerbils also have scent glands in their abdomen and on their neck.

Gerbil, above and facing page

BATs

(Order: Chiroptera)

Glossophagine bat

If we lost our sense of smell, we'd miss the smell of the earth after a rainstorm or cookies baking in the oven, but we'd survive just the same. If a fruit-eating bat lost its sense of smell, it would die. Unlike insect-eating bats that depend solely upon their sense of hearing to find food, fruit-eating bats rely on their keen sense of smell.

Bats may look like a cross between a rodent and a bird, but they are mammals, the only mammals that fly. The original reason mammals developed a sharp sense of smell was so they could feed at night and avoid becoming food for dinosaurs, which hunted during the day. Fruit-eating bats are relatives of those first mammals who began smelling their way to food in the dark because it was safer. The olfactory lobe—the area of the brain that processes smells—of a fruit bat is significantly larger than that of an insect-eating bat. Fruit bats feed at night and follow their nose to the tropical fruits they love: guavas, figs, bananas, and mangoes.

Fruit bats are strong fliers and sometimes travel long distances to feast at their favorite feeding areas. They have a hearty appetite and often will eat the equivalent of their own weight in fruit in a single evening.

There *is* one thing that can impair a bat's ability to smell its way to food: wind. On windy nights when smells are blown away, fruit-eating bats go hungry.

THE RIPE CHOICE

Fruit-eating bats are frugivores, meaning they eat only fruit. (Insectivores eat insects, herbivores eat plants, carnivores eat meat, and omnivores—like us—eat just about anything!) Even in the dark, without feeling the fruit, the frugivorous bat knows the difference between a ripe guava and one that is not yet ready to eat. By smell alone, the bat will select only the ripest fruit, leaving the unripe fruit to mature for a later meal.

Fruit-eating bats rely on their keen sense of smell to locate ripe tropical fruits.

Gothic bat, facing page

SNAKes

(Order: Squamata)

Green-headed racer

Many snakes find their prey by smelling the trail that the creature leaves behind it. This hunting technique is called trailing. Different kinds of snakes trail different kinds of food. The rat snake, for example, follows the scent of rodents, while the garter snake in your garden sniffs after insects. The American blind snake also tracks its favorite food, ants, by sense of smell. Humans taste many foods before deciding what we like best. But snakes know by instinct what prey suits them, as well as its distinct scent.

Trailing requires a keen sense of smell. Snakes have nostrils, the holes in the nose that let in air. But they also have a special organ on the roof of their mouth that aids them in smelling prey. This is called the Jacobson's organ. The snake uses this organ by flicking its tongue in and out of its mouth. When the tongue is out of the mouth, it picks up scent molecules hanging in the air. When it darts back in the mouth, it rubs these molecules onto the Jacobson's organ. From there, the sensory impulses are carried to the snake's brain, which interprets what the smell is and tells the snake what action to take. Snakes also flicker their tongues when they sense danger and are preparing to strike. If you come across a snake doing this, you should excuse yourself—fast!

FEEL THE HEAT

Unlike many snakes, the rattlesnake does not trail its prey. It uses a heat-sensitive organ called a pit organ to hunt warm-blooded prey, whose warm bodies slightly change the temperature of the air around them. Pit organs are cavities in the snake's head, usually in front of and under the eyes. When the rattlesnake finds it prey (a mouse, for example), it bites it, injecting venom, and then lets it go. As the poisoned mouse tries to escape, the rattlesnake tracks its dying victim by following the warmth of the mouse's body, as well as the scent of its own venom.

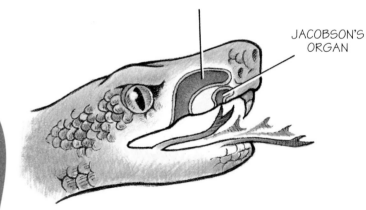

NASAL CAVITY

JACOBSON'S ORGAN

When snakes flicker their tongues, they are actually bringing scent molecules from the air to the smelling organ on the roof of their mouth.

Black-tailed rattlesnake, facing page

Kiwis

(*Apteryx australis*)

New Zealand's kiwi may look like a feathered football with a soda straw nose, but in the world of birds it is a very special creature. About the size of a chicken, the kiwi has no tail, bad eyesight, and tiny little wings that won't even lift it off the ground.

But the kiwi has something no other bird has: the ability to smell worms *underground*. This is an important skill for a bird whose diet consists of earthworms and burrowing insects. By day these shy, shaggy birds hide in the forest underbrush. At night they leave their hiding places and become mighty earthworm hunters, poking and probing the forest floor for the juicy worms they love.

Other birds have nostrils close to their heads and locate their prey by seeing or feeling it. Birds such as starlings or waders feed by probing for buried insects, just as the kiwi does. But these other birds find their food by digging a hole in the ground and peering down their bills for their hidden meal. The kiwi alone can smell insects underground.

Unlike every other bird's, the kiwi's nostrils are at the tip of its bill. How do kiwis snuffle in the soil without getting a snoutful of dirt? No one knows for sure, but the hair-like feathers at the base of its bill probably help. Like whiskers on mammals, they may keep the kiwi out of too-tight spots. Or, like our nose hairs, they may filter out dirt particles as the kiwi sniffs around in the earth.

MIND YOUR OWN BEESWAX

Besides the kiwi, the only other insect-eating bird known to rely heavily on its sense of smell is the African honey guide. A Portuguese missionary in East Africa discovered this when he lit some beeswax candles. The unlit candles attracted no birds. But when the priest lit the candles, the church was soon filled with the small birds. (Why? Because smells are intensified by heat.) The honey guides flew right up to the candles—and *ate* the warm wax!

Kiwis dine on burrowing insects and earthworms. They are the only birds able to smell insects underground.

Brown kiwi, above and facing page

Prairie Dogs

(Genus: *Cynomys*)

Prairie dogs, so-named for their bark-like call, are among the most sociable of creatures. These rodents live in large colonies, and their social structure is organized around the sense of smell. A prairie dog town may have as many as thirty districts, and each district houses a clan of about forty members. The walls of a prairie dog town are invisible to the human eye, but not to the prairie dog nose. These walls are all scent boundaries that mark borders.

It is important for an individual prairie dog to be good at smelling these boundaries, because it is strictly forbidden to cross over into unfamiliar territory. In fact, if a prairie dog does cross a scent boundary, whether on purpose or by mistake, the unlucky animal will immediately be attacked by the whole family of invaded prairie dogs. These scent boundaries give off a definite message: visitors are not welcome.

Sometimes a prairie dog gets the urge to ignore these invisible "No Trespassing" signs. Most often, it is the bold young males who want to explore unfamiliar territory. But the adventurous youth doesn't just use force. He may actually try to make friends first, so he'll have some allies in the new neighborhood. He does this by flirting with the females. If all goes well and he is allowed into the new camp, some of these females may become his mates.

Whitetail prairie dog

BORDER PATROL

Female prairie dogs also patrol scent boundaries. If a female trespasses, a resident may cautiously approach her and show her teeth. In effect, she is asking the stranger to show her "passport." The visitor may raise her tail, showing her scent glands. But the wrong scent can set off a battle, with both prairie dogs biting and running. The fight will end when both pick up the scent of the boundary line and retreat to their own side.

Prairie dogs mark their territory with scent boundaries. If a prairie dog from another neighborhood tries to cross this invisible border, a resident will most likely threaten or attack the intruder.

Black-tailed prairie dog, facing page

Cats

(Family: Felidae)

A cat's petite nose is actually the smallest part of its keen olfactory system. Behind its nose is a maze of bone and cavities that contains a lining with 200 million olfactory cells. As the cat breathes, air is warmed, moistened, and passed across this lining and over the olfactory cells. Signals are then sent to the olfactory lobe of the cat's brain, which interprets the smells.

Cats have a reputation for being finicky about their food. But it is actually the smell of meat, rather than the taste, that cats react to. A cat who doesn't like liver, for example, really doesn't like the *smell* of liver and will refuse to eat it. In fact, if a cat has a cold and can't smell, it won't eat because it can't be sure its food is actually food.

Cats, like dogs, have two openings in the roof of the mouth lined with olfactory cells. This is called the vomeronasal organ, and it is very similar to the snake's Jacobson's organ. You've probably seen a cat stretch its neck, open its mouth, and curl its lips in a funny smile. What it's doing is bringing air to the vomeronasal organ for a good whiff, just as snakes flicker their tongue to rub scent molecules on their Jacobson's organ. Cats mostly use their sense of smell to locate and investigate stationary objects, such as their food dish or an intoxicating ball of catnip.

Ocelot

HEADS OR TAILS

Cats have glands in various parts of their bodies that secrete pheromones. These leave scent messages for other animals about the cat's territory and its catty activities. One area with scent glands is the forehead. When your cat rubs its head against your legs or against the living room couch, it is marking its territory and making it familiar with its own smell. Cats use smell as a form of greeting, first going nose to nose and then turning around and lifting their tails. Your cat may do this to you, too—probably not the best way to say "how do you do?" in a human social setting, but it's very good manners in the cat world.

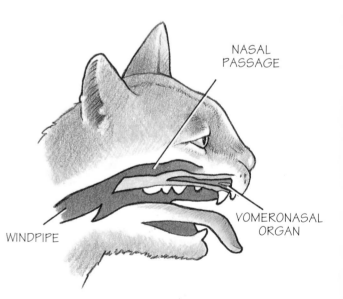

NASAL PASSAGE

VOMERONASAL ORGAN

WINDPIPE

Cats have two openings in the roof of the mouth lined with olfactory cells. This is called the vomeronasal organ, and it is very similar to the snake's Jacobson's organ.

146

Asian lion, facing page

Salmon

(Genera: *Salmo* and *Oncorhynchus*)

Salmon go far with their noses—really far. Without a map or a compass, a salmon will travel as many as 1,000 miles from the ocean back to the river of its birth, using only its nose for navigation.

A salmon's sense of smell is very sensitive, picking up even the faintest of odors. The fish's nose is made up of two separate openings, called olfactory pits, connected by a pair of U-shaped tubes. Water flows in through the first opening while the salmon swims and breathes, then flows out through the second opening. Odors in the water stimulate the olfactory receptors—cells that receive smells—which send information to the salmon's brain. A salmon's nose is not connected to its throat and mouth, like ours is. Instead, it is attached to an area of its brain that evaluates the smells in water.

Shortly after a salmon hatches in the freshwater of a mountain stream, it swims down into the ocean. As many as seven years later, it begins the long trip home. For two to three weeks, it swims day and night without eating or sleeping. Moving along at $2^{1}/_{2}$ to $4^{1}/_{2}$ miles per hour, the fish swims hundreds of miles through the ocean and up a series of rivers to the exact river it was born in. Once salmon reach their home waters, they lay and fertilize their eggs, and then die. This dramatic rite of nature is called the spawning of salmon.

Salmo fontinalis

LED BY THE NOSE

Salmon are drawn homeward by the smell of their home waters and the smell of young salmon in the river or stream where they were born. Their keen sense of smell also alerts them to trouble. The skin of an injured fish gives off a scent that warns other fish of danger.

Swimming upriver against the current, salmon sometimes have to launch themselves into the air to climb waterfalls.

Red salmon, facing page

Lemurs

(Family: Lemuridae)

Ring-tailed lemur

The lemur is a small monkey-like creature that, along with humans, is a primate. Lemurs live on the island of Madagascar, off the east coast of Africa. The ring-tailed lemur has a most impressive tail, striped like a raccoon's and bushy as a squirrel's. Lemurs are among the most ancient of animals. They swing from the trees at all levels of the forest.

The lemur has a well-developed olfactory center in its brain. Like the skunk, the lemur has musk glands that secrete a very foul odor. The main purpose of the lemur's odor is to communicate with other lemurs.

The male lemur has musk glands on its tail and fore-arms. To mark its territory, the lemur rubs its strong scent on twigs and anything else it happens to pass on its forest rounds. When a male prepares to do battle with other males during the mating season, he drags his tail across his musk glands over and over again, covering the tail with scent. The tail then becomes his not-so-secret weapon as he waves it in the breeze to ward off other males. The lemur's waving black-and-white ringed tail is first a visual warning signal. When it is permeated with scent, it becomes a definite "Do Not Enter" sign. Because their tails are so important to them, lemurs comb them often with a special grooming claw on the second digit (toe) of each foot.

SCENT STAND

Why do lemurs stand on their head? These animals do headstands to press their rear ends against a tree trunk. In a zoo, they will do it against the wall of a cage. This is another way of marking territory with scent. The gray gentle lemur is similar to the ring-tailed lemur. Its upper arms have glands that secrete a liquid that is milky-white and smells like beeswax. Not only lemurs can smell this; humans too can pick up the scent from neighboring tree trunks.

During the mating season, male lemurs cover their tails with a foul scent from their musk glands and wave them in the breeze to ward off other males.

Collared lemur, facing page

150

SAlamanders

(Order: Caudata)

A salamander may look like a lizard, but it is not. It lacks both the claws and scales that characterize lizards. Like the frog, the salamander is an amphibian, an animal that lives both in water and on land. Salamanders depend upon their noses to find a good meal, such as a small worm or some shellfish

The Texas blind salamander, creeping around in dark caves, searches for its food by using its sense of smell. In the Ozark mountains of Arkansas lives the Grotto salamander. (A grotto is a cave, this salamander's natural habitat.) Like its cousin in Texas, it too sniffs out its food and has little use for good vision. In fact, skin grows over their eyes as salamanders mature. Most salamanders have nostrils and nasal cavities similar to humans'. The animal inhales airborne odors, and olfactory receptors in the nasal cavity detect them.

But other types of salamanders don't have such conventional noses. They don't even have lungs. They breathe and smell through their skin! Oxygen passes directly through their moist, flexible, thin skin.

Salamanders use their sense of smell for more than food. During the mating season, male and female salamanders smell for each other. They have special glands that become active during the mating season. Different types of salamanders have these glands on different parts of their bodies. Some have them on the head and chin, others on the tail, and still others on the abdomen.

Red-spotted newt

MATING MATCH

During the mating season, salamanders behave rather oddly. A male and female face each other. They tap each other on the nose. Then they touch each other on the chin. They look like they're throwing a few good punches in a salamander boxing match! They do this only during the mating season, after their glands start to secrete. This strange ritual allows the salamanders to check each other out before mating.

Some species of salamander breathe and smell through their thin, flexible skin.

Long-tailed salamander, facing page

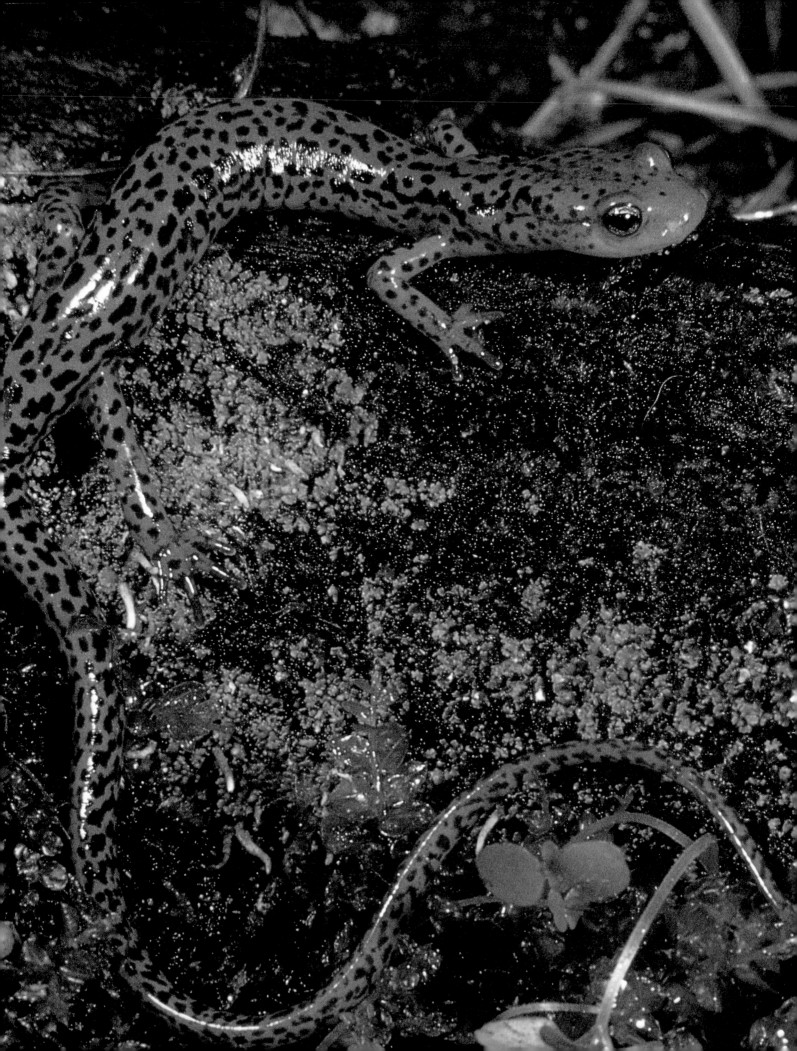

DOGS

(Canis familiaris)

Bernese mountain dog

When a dog twitches and barks in its sleep, we sometimes say it's dreaming about chasing rabbits. But dogs don't dream about the rabbits themselves, they dream about their smell. Dogs "see" the world with their noses. In fact, the largest part of a dog's brain is devoted to interpreting smells.

Dogs' long snouts have 10 to 15 times more area for sensory cells than our noses do. The inside of a dog's nose is lined with up to 200 million olfactory receptor cells. Like cats, dogs also smell through two small openings on the roof of their mouth, called the vomeronasal organ.

You can act tough in front of a growling dog, but it will probably know you're scared anyway. This is because dogs can smell moods. Strong emotions produce chemical reactions in our bodies. Humans usually can't detect these subtle scents, but dogs aren't fooled.

Dogs "talk" to each other by leaving scent messages behind for other dogs to "read." Pockets between the pads of their paws leave a scent trail on the ground that can last for days. And you've probably seen the neighborhood dog relieving itself on every bush on the street. This is its way of marking territory. A dog's urine reveals its age, whether it's male or female, whether it's the poodle next door or the spaniel across the tracks, and whether it was excited, frightened, or hostile when it passed by. The ground around your neighborhood is your dog's newspaper, providing it with all the information it needs to know about what's going on in its world.

P.S. Just as no two people have identical fingerprints, each dog has a unique nose print.

HOT ON THE TRAIL

Their powerful sense of smell and willingness to serve makes dogs very good workers, as well as wonderful companions. German shepherds and other breeds help police by sniffing out illegal substances or tracking criminals on the run. Other dogs work with rescue teams to find lost or injured people.

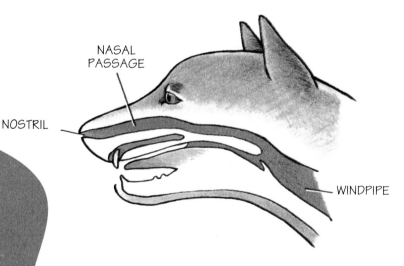

NASAL PASSAGE

NOSTRIL

WINDPIPE

Dogs have 10 to 15 times more smelling area inside their noses than humans do.

Shar pei, facing page

Turkey Vultures

(Cathartes aura)

With their bare, red heads, dark feathers, and hunched posture, turkey vultures aren't very pretty to look at. But these birds have keen eyes and can see their prey from great distances. It is their powerful sense of smell, however, that sets them apart from other birds.

These large birds, found from southern Canada to South America, are scavengers, which means they eat dead animals. It's a dirty job, but somebody's got to do it, and turkey vultures seem content to serve as the sanitation workers of the animal kindgom. Although they do take live prey if it is available, turkey vultures most often dine on dead animals (called carrion) and garbage. By eating carrion, vultures perform the useful service of disposing of decaying material that might otherwise be a breeding ground for dangerous bacteria.

Believe it or not, turkey vultures have been known to lend a helping hand—or rather, nose—to people. These birds gather around areas where underground fuel pipes have fractured, attracted by the chemical used to give natural gas an odor. The turkey vulture's powerful sense of smell can lead engineers to a gas leak much more quickly than their own laborious search would.

Turkey vultures, also called buzzards, are powerful, graceful fliers. They spend much of their time soaring high in the air, looking for food. As they fly over the land, odors given off by a dead animal alert the turkey vulture that a meal might be nearby. The vulture circles in the air, drawn closer and closer by the smell of decaying carrion.

A REAL STEAL

Turkey vultures are well-liked by other members of the vulture family, but not for their wonderful personalities. The turkey vulture's cousins—the North American black vulture, the American condor, and the California condor— can't smell worth a hoot, so they rely on the turkey vulture's keen sense of smell to help them find food. The cousins watch the turkey vulture's hunting flights, using the bird as a scout. Once it finds food, the cousin vultures descend on the bird and steal its meal.

The turkey vulture circles in the air over the carrion on which it feeds. It is drawn closer and closer by the smell of decaying flesh.

Turkey vulture, above and facing page

Sharks

(Order: Squaliformes)

Sand tiger shark

Imagine not using your nose to breathe, but only to find food. That's what a shark does. Sharks are carnivores (meat-eaters) and hunt their prey, mostly other fish, by scent. This is called chemosensing, detecting chemical reactions with sensory organs. A blindfolded shark can locate dead crabs in less than a minute. Because it depends on smell for survival, the olfactory lobes in a shark's brain are very large. By contrast, the optic lobes, which process sight, are small because vision is not very important to the shark.

Sharks often hunt injured prey. They can smell a single drop of blood in 25 gallons of water—about the amount it would take to fill a small wading pool—and an injured fish will bleed a lot more than a drop. Sharks also pursue healthy, active fish, especially if the fish are agitated and give off a stronger than usual scent.

A shark can follow an odor trail very precisely, tracking exactly the path of a fish swimming ahead, out of sight. Sharks have been known to attack humans, particularly injured swimmers or divers. Even a small amount of blood in the water can attract a shark from a considerable distance—unless it's shark blood, that is. The smell of injured shark triggers an alarm reaction in other sharks and they stay away.

Sharks are often called the "hounds of the sea" because their noses are as sensitive as a dog's. Another of their nicknames is the "swimming nose."

MAN-EATING SHARKS

Terrifying movies have been made about sharks attacking bathers at the beach, but such attacks seldom happen. Generally, sharks stay out of the shallow water where people are most likely to go swimming. As more people venture into deeper waters with scuba equipment, shark attacks are becoming more common.

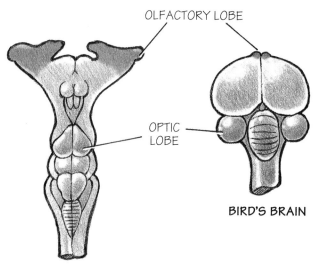

OLFACTORY LOBE

OPTIC LOBE

SHARK'S BRAIN

BIRD'S BRAIN

The olfactory lobes in a shark's brain are very large compared to the optic lobe, which handles sight. By contrast, the olfactory lobes in a bird's brain are just two little nubs.

158

Great white shark, facing page

ELEPHANTS

(Elephas maximus or Loxodonta africana)

The elephant has the biggest nose in the world, and no wonder: it is the largest land mammal of all. Elephants have a very keen sense of smell, which is a good thing since they do not see very well. They use their sense of smell to locate food, find mates, and detect enemies. When a herd of wild elephants is out walking together they may pause suddenly, their trunks swaying, and then lift them to sniff the air all together.

An elephant's sense of smell is so sensitive it can detect the scent of a human being three miles away. Unfortunately, their sense of smell is no protection against big game hunters and ivory collectors, who have hunted these intelligent creatures so heavily they are now endangered species.

Elephants are very sociable creatures, and they use their sense of smell to keep track of their family members. Elephants leave something for each other to smell; they have glands on their faces that release scents used for marking territory and for attracting a mate. When an elephant smells the ground or trees, it is figuring out which of its neighbors or family members has passed by.

The elephant's nose is far more than just an organ of smell. Asian elephants are so dexterous with their trunk, they can pick up an object as tiny as a coin. Elephants are very affectionate and loyal, but they lack arms for hugging. This doesn't stop them: elephant parents hug their children with their trunks.

Asiatic elephant

TRUNK PRACTICE

A baby elephant, called a calf, does not have the use of its trunk. The trunk just hangs from the calf's head, floppy and useless. Like a human child, it must learn coordination. The first thing the calf discovers about its trunk is that it can suck on the tip of it, just as human infants suck their thumbs. After about three months, the young elephant begins to learn all the varied uses of this invaluable organ.

Elephants hold their trunks high like flags when they sniff the air.

African elephant, facing page

GUSTATORY GUSTO

You probably have favorite foods, as well as foods you can't stand. Other animals also have food preferences. Mostly, these likes and dislikes are innate, which means the animals are born knowing what food suits them. But some animals acquire a taste for a particular food, which is another way of saying they learn to like it. For example, canines in the wild would never eat potato chips or cookies, but it doesn't take much coaxing to get your dog to share yours. Your pet has learned to eat human foods—and probably with gusto!

In humans, the sense of taste (also called **gustation**) detects four basic tastes: **bitter**, **salty**, **sweet**, and **sour**. Many animals have a powerful sweet tooth, including humans. You have probably been warned not to eat too much sugar—it adds little nutrition to your diet and is bad for your teeth. But for many animals, sugar is the key to their survival. Honeybees,

Our sense of taste helps us select foods we need and like, and avoid substances that are harmful to us, such as spoiled food and sour milk.

butterflies, and other insects get their energy from sugar sources such as flowers. Sugar from flowers? Yes, the nectar in flowering plants contains sucrose. Humans process sucrose from cane and beets to make table sugar. There are other kinds of sugar as well. Lactose is the sugar present in mammals' milk. Fructose is found in honey and many fruits. And glucose, not as sweet as ordinary sugar, is present in animal tissue and some fruits.

But some animals are indifferent to any type of sugar. They crave other tastes instead. Herbivores (plant-eaters) such as deer and giraffes, for example, will travel miles to lick salty earth. Few animals are fond of a bitter flavor, although dolphins don't seem to mind it. Humans are most sensitive to this taste, probably because bitter things are often poisonous, and we know instinctively to avoid them. Our taste buds for bitter are located at the back of our tongue. There, they stand guard against our swallowing dangerous substances.

Different animals have different taste preferences. Honeybees and butterflies have a real sweet tooth, while sheep, cows, and other plant-eating animals crave salt. Many farmers put out a salt block for their livestock.

Tongue Types

Not all organs of taste are alike—far from it. Blowflies and butterflies taste with their feet, minnows with their lips, cockroaches with their antennae and mouth parts, and catfish with their whole body! The most common taste organ in higher animals is the tongue, of course, and these too come in all shapes and sizes. Your tongue is relatively small, flat, and inflexible, especially compared with the tongues of frogs, chameleons, and woodpeckers. These animals have long, protrusible tongues, which means they can stick far out of the animal's mouth. The famous flicking, forked tongues of lizards and snakes work together with a sense organ in the animals' mouth to detect tastes and smells. The anteater's long tongue probes deep into termite tunnels, traps the insects in its sticky coating, and then grinds them to pieces against the roof of the animal's mouth.

SPICY ADVENTURES

Would you travel halfway around the world to make your food taste better? It sounds far-fetched, but the great wave of European exploration during the 1400s was fueled in part by people's appetite for exotic tastes. European navigators sought an all-water trade route to distant Asia so they could gain access to gold, silk, gems, and spices. The Spice Islands of the Indian Ocean—so-named for the cinnamon, nutmeg, cloves, mace, pepper, and ginger that grew there—became the crossroads of a bustling international trade. In fact, Christopher Columbus was on his way to the Spice Islands when he stumbled upon the New World by accident. Today, many people are still eager for new gustatory experiences. How would you like to gnaw on the tentacles of an octopus? Or eat grasshoppers coated with carob? Or snack on a snake steak? In some parts of the world, these are considered tasty treats. Food preferences are shaped as much by our culture and the availability of certain foods as they are by the 10,000 or so taste buds on our tongues.

A Taste Sensation

You can see, hear, and smell things from a distance. But rarely can you taste something far away. That's because taste is a contact sense, meaning a substance must actually touch our taste buds before we can detect its flavor. (A few animals *can* taste from a distance. You'll read about them soon.)

No matter the type of taste organ—antennae, foot, skin, or tongue—taste sensation is possible because of cells called **chemoreceptors**. Chemoreceptors receive the tiny chemical particles that give food and other substances their taste. When chemoreceptors are stimulated, they send electrical impulses to the brain. The brain interprets the impulses as taste and tells the animal what to do in response to them. If the brain understands the taste as food, for example, it will direct the animal to eat. If the brain interprets the substance as harmful or unpleasant, it will tell the animal to reject it.

Throughout the animal kingdom, the sense of taste is often directly linked to the sense of smell. In fact, for the lobster, the organs for taste and smell are the same.

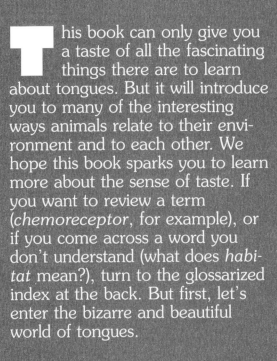

This book can only give you a taste of all the fascinating things there are to learn about tongues. But it will introduce you to many of the interesting ways animals relate to their environment and to each other. We hope this book sparks you to learn more about the sense of taste. If you want to review a term (*chemoreceptor*, for example), or if you come across a word you don't understand (what does *habitat* mean?), turn to the glossarized index at the back. But first, let's enter the bizarre and beautiful world of tongues.

In part, the age of European exploration was fueled by people's hearty appetite for spices and seasonings.

EARThwORMS

(Order: Terricolae)

A gooey, segmented earthworm creeping through the mud after a rainstorm is a common sight. In fact, there are over 1,800 species of earthworms worldwide. How does this weird and primitive creature, with no recognizable eyes, ears, or sense organs, find food and shelter?

In the late 1800s, the famous naturalist Charles Darwin observed that earthworms could easily distinguish between different foods and chemicals. He found that, given a choice, earthworms were terribly picky eaters. An earthworm will ignore cabbage if celery is also offered, and refuse celery if carrot leaves are available (an earthworm favorite!). It will even select green leaves over brown ones from the same tree. The earthworm's body is covered with simple taste-sensitive cells, called chemoreceptors, that taste the substance the animal is touching. Around the earthworm's mouth, or prostomium, are over 700 taste receptors that detect sweet substances. This area is only one square millimeter—about the size of a crumb!

Earthworms also use their sense of taste to find each other. During mating season earthworms secrete a milky fluid. By following the taste of this milky trail earthworms are able to locate each other from a distance.

Humans can taste sweet, sour, bitter, and salty substances, but earthworms can also taste acids. This ability is essential to their survival because earthworms die in soil with too much acid in it. When the acid concentration becomes too high, the earthworm will emerge from its burrow in a frenzy and quickly search for less acidic soil.

WONDERFUL WORM!

Before you write off the earthworm as just another slimy bug, consider the good work these creatures do. Earthworms are born soil cultivators. As they burrow into the ground they circulate layers of soil and create tunnels in the earth. This loosens the soil, makes it more fertile, and allows roots to seek nourishment deep in the ground. In fact, farmers often report better crops when earthworms are present in the soil.

The earthworm's body is covered with cells called chemoreceptors that taste whatever the worm is touching.

Common earthworm, above and facing page

164

Bees

(Order: Hymenoptera)

Bees have a sweet tooth—or rather, a sweet tongue. But many things that taste sweet to us are tasteless to bees, such as saccharin, an artificial sweetener. What really makes bees buzz are the natural sugars found in their favorite foods, nectar and honeydew, a sweet substance that seeps out of certain leaves in hot weather. Flowers are adapted to the bee's love of sugar, and together the plant and the insect form a perfect partnership. The flower secretes nectar at the base of its blossom, and the bee helps pollinate the flower on its way to gather the nectar.

How do bees locate a nectar harvest? By using their senses of smell and taste, which are linked in many animals. Bees have taste cones on their jaws, and they also seem able to taste with their tongues, forelegs, and antennae. And that's not all. Some scientists believe bees can also taste with their proboscises, the slender beaks through which they feed. Imagine if you had taste buds on your knees, nose, and ears, as well as on your tongue! On the bee, it makes sense that these body parts are taste-sensitive because they are all involved in gathering nectar and pollen.

The honeybee's favorite taste is sweetness, but it can also taste salty, bitter, and sour flavors. But bees are unlikely to be attracted to your salted peanuts or popcorn. In fact, if salt is added to a bee's sugary meal, the insect will reject it. If a bee is really hungry, it may drink a mixture that is slightly bitter, but it will never take to something sweet that is mixed with salt.

Bumblebee

HOW SWEET IT IS

Honeybees are sensitive to the sweetness of the nectar they find. The sweeter the nectar, the more of it a bee will collect. There's a good reason for this. Sugar acts as a preservative. So the sweeter the nectar, the more likely it will last the winter stored in a honeycomb.

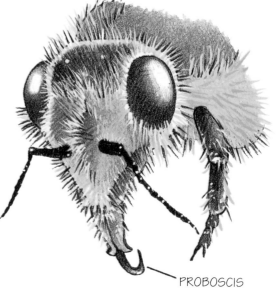

PROBOSCIS

Some scientists think that the bee is able to taste with its proboscis (beak), as well as its antennae, tongue, and forelegs.

Buff-tailed bumblebee, facing page

166

Blowflies

(Family: Calliphoridae)

When a blowfly lands on your plate and walks over your meal, it is actually taste-testing your food—with its feet! At each foot's tip, or tarsus, are cells that receive chemical information from the fly's environment. These cells are called chemoreceptors. Tiny hairs on the fly's feet serve as chemoreceptors for taste. They send information to the blowfly's brain, which then tells the insect whether to investigate the substance or leave it alone.

Like the bee, the blowfly is most interested in sucrose (table sugar). When the tarsal hairs detect sucrose, the blowfly's coiled beak automatically unwinds and sticks out straight. This beak is called a proboscis and works like a straw to suck up food. At the end of the proboscis is a spongy pad called the labellum, which is also covered with chemoreceptive hairs. The labellum pokes the substance, and if it detects sucrose it spreads open to reveal even more chemoreceptive hairs. These hairs prompt the fly to begin feeding.

Blowflies also have sensory hairs on their mouth parts. At the base of these hairs are two taste cells. One is sensitive to salts, acids, and alcohols, and the other detects sugar. These sensory cells send electrical impulses to the blowfly's brain, which determines whether the substance is suitable or unsuitable for blowfly dining. Only sweet tastes will whet the appetite of a blowfly.

SUGAR FIENDS

A blowfly's taste cells indicate "sweet," "not sweet," and also "how sweet?" Hair cells detecting sucrose send different messages to the brain depending on the kind of sugar. Some cells send impulses for low concentrations of sugar and others for high concentrations. What look like simple hairs on the outside of the fly's body are actually complex receptors that gather and pass on a lot of information.

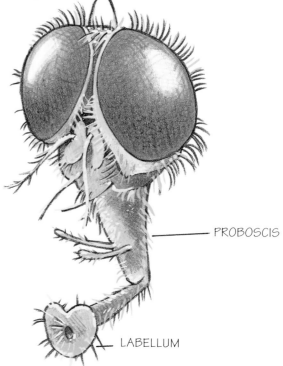

— PROBOSCIS

— LABELLUM

The spongy pad at the end of the blowfly's proboscis is called the labellum. It is covered with tiny hairs that detect taste.

Green-bottle fly, above and facing page

COCKROACHES

(Suborder: Blattaria)

Madagascar hissing cockroaches

Cockroaches are nocturnal insects that have remained almost unchanged for over 200 million years. They are remarkably adaptable insects and will eat even dry wood and paper if no other food is available. Such flexibility has enabled these creepy critters to survive in virtually all parts of the world—including kitchens! However, although they are notorious household pests, less than two percent of cockroaches actually dwell side by side with humans. Most thrive in rain forests where they dart in and out of small crevices to avoid being eaten by other animals.

Cockroaches sense chemicals in their environment with cells called chemoreceptors. Generally, both odors and tastes are detected by chemoreceptors. But olfactory (smell) chemoreceptors identify chemicals that are far away. Taste chemoreceptors identify only chemicals in high concentration, or those actually touched. Taste and smell are so similar in many animals, it is often hard to tell which of the two senses is at work. Cockroaches use both of these senses to locate their midnight feasts. For example, if a banana is placed across the room from a cockroach, the insect will skitter about trying to follow the scent of the fruit. Once the treasure is discovered—bananas are a cockroach delicacy—the cockroach tastes the fruit with its antennae and mouth parts before eating. Cockroaches also use their senses of smell and taste to communicate with each other. During mating season, the female emits a perfume called a pheromone to attract the male. But the male cockroach will court the female only if he is able to taste the pheromone as well as smell it. Cockroaches taste with thousands of sensory hairs located on their antennae and mouth parts. Some of these hairs can taste only a specific substance, such as salt. But most of the hairs can taste sweet, sour, salty, and bitter substances.

TASTEFUL CHOICES

Taste is important because it helps an animal find the specific ingredients lacking in its diet. For example, if a cockroach needs sugar, it will be able to identify a substance as sweet and gorge itself accordingly.

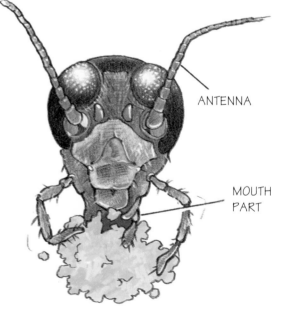

ANTENNA

MOUTH PART

Cockroaches taste with thousands of sensory hairs located on their antennae and mouth parts.

Giant cockroach, facing page

170

Butterflies

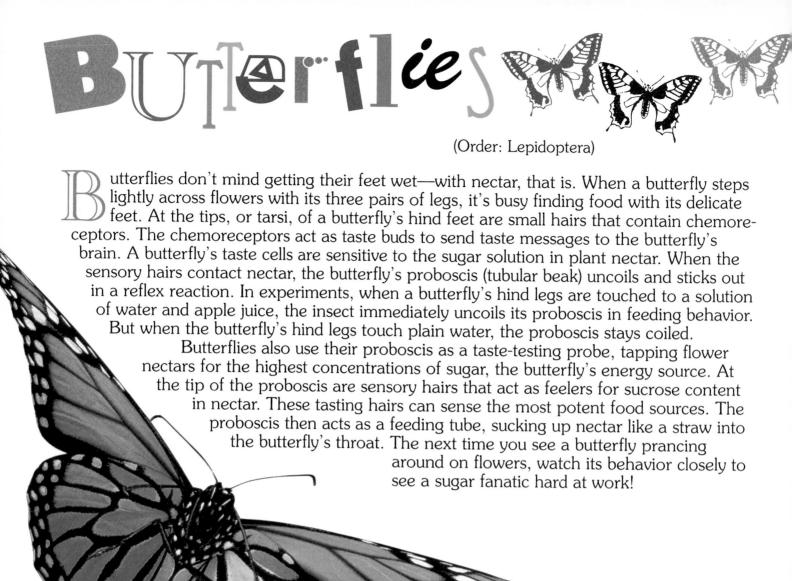

(Order: Lepidoptera)

Butterflies don't mind getting their feet wet—with nectar, that is. When a butterfly steps lightly across flowers with its three pairs of legs, it's busy finding food with its delicate feet. At the tips, or tarsi, of a butterfly's hind feet are small hairs that contain chemoreceptors. The chemoreceptors act as taste buds to send taste messages to the butterfly's brain. A butterfly's taste cells are sensitive to the sugar solution in plant nectar. When the sensory hairs contact nectar, the butterfly's proboscis (tubular beak) uncoils and sticks out in a reflex reaction. In experiments, when a butterfly's hind legs are touched to a solution of water and apple juice, the insect immediately uncoils its proboscis in feeding behavior. But when the butterfly's hind legs touch plain water, the proboscis stays coiled.

Butterflies also use their proboscis as a taste-testing probe, tapping flower nectars for the highest concentrations of sugar, the butterfly's energy source. At the tip of the proboscis are sensory hairs that act as feelers for sucrose content in nectar. These tasting hairs can sense the most potent food sources. The proboscis then acts as a feeding tube, sucking up nectar like a straw into the butterfly's throat. The next time you see a butterfly prancing around on flowers, watch its behavior closely to see a sugar fanatic hard at work!

Monarch butterfly

MULTIPURPOSE LEGS

Attached to the upper-middle part of a butterfly's body (the thorax) are three pairs of legs. These legs are used primarily for walking and climbing over flowers when the butterfly is looking for nectar. Tiny claws at the ends of the legs are used for clinging while the butterfly roosts, mates, or drys its wings. But the rear legs serve another purpose, too. They detect taste through the chemoreceptive hairs on their tips.

The butterfly uncoils its proboscis to probe flowers for nectar. The slender beak also serves as a feeding tube, sucking up nectar like a straw.

Eye and coiled proboscis of Gulf fritillary butterfly, facing page

CRUSTACEANS

(Class: Crustacea)

Crustaceans are aquatic, or water-dwelling, creatures with segmented legs. Like spiders and insects, they are invertebrates, animals without a backbone. Instead of spines, crustaceans have hard outer shells (exoskeletons) for support. Lobsters, crabs, shrimp, and other crustaceans taste with the chemoreceptors on their antennae, legs, and mouth parts. These chemoreceptors are hair-like organs that detect the presence of certain food chemicals in the aquatic environment.

The sense organs for taste and smell are the same in crustaceans. However, some of these hair-like chemoreceptors detect chemicals at a distance, and some detect only certain chemicals. Clusters of these hairs on both the long and short antennae of a lobster, for instance, first sense food at a distance. These chemoreceptors are considered organs of smell. A lobster will flick its antennae in the presence of food chemicals to increase the sensation to chemoreceptors. Sensory cells in the receptor hairs send signals to the nervous system and the lobster begins feeding behavior: it starts to walk and to move the appendages near its mouth. Tiny hairs on these appendages also detect the chemicals and help lead the animal to their source.

There are also clusters of sense hairs on the lobster's finger-like legs. These chemoreceptors are considered organs of taste. They are sensitive to the amino acids given off by prey swimming nearby. (Amino acids are the building blocks of proteins.) When the lobster detects these amino acids, it reaches and grasps for food, its legs drawing the captured food to the mouth. Some of the lobster's mouth parts are also taste-senstive. They contain groups of long hairs that send taste messages to the lobster's nervous system. Shrimp, crabs, and crayfish have organs of taste similar to the lobster's.

Fiddler crab

HOW SHRIMP TASTES

To many people and marine animals, shrimp are mighty tasty. But these tiny crustaceans have a *sense* of taste as well. How do we know? In experiments, shrimp respond to meat juice that touches their legs or mouth parts. They react with a fast grasping motion. This is called feeding behavior and is evidence of taste sensation.

Like many crustaceans, lobsters taste with the chemoreceptive hairs on their legs and mouth parts.

Red hermit crab, facing page

Minnows

(Phoxinus phoxinus)

F ish have been around for more than 400 million years, since the Paleozoic era. Compare that with how long humans in our current form have walked the Earth—only 40,000 years or so! These ancient creatures have had plenty of time to develop their senses, and minnows have an especially keen sense of taste. This small, swift fish has taste buds on its lips, head, and body.

Minnows rely on their super sense of taste to locate food and to avoid substances that are harmful to them. In minnows, as in many animals, the senses of taste and smell work together. The sensor cells on the minnow's body help the fish gauge the distance of the food source. The closer the minnow gets to the food, the stronger the scent and taste.

Minnows have nerve endings under their skin. These nerve endings break into tiny branches and then divide into even narrower endings. This network of specialized cells is very sensitive. Some respond to chemicals, while others are tuned to temperature. Nerve endings that are sensitive to chemicals and temperature are probably the narrower ones. The bigger endings are probably tactile, which means they detect touch. Nerves that respond to tactile, temperature, and chemical sensation work together very closely in the minnow's skin.

Sheepshead minnow

TASTE PROS

Minnows recognize some tastes much more accurately than humans can. In fact, they identify certain sugars (lactose and fructose) thousands of times better than humans do. Lactose is the sugar present in milk, and fructose is sugar found in honey and many kinds of fruit.

Minnows have taste-sensitive cells on their lips, heads, and bodies.

Bluntnose minnow, facing page

FROGS

(Order: Anura)

Frogs are amphibians, animals that can live both on land and in water. But young frogs, called tadpoles, cannot live outside of water. During a process called metamorphosis, tadpoles absorb their tales, grow legs, and develop the ability to breathe air.

But what does all of this have to do with the frog's tongue? Eons ago, amphibians evolved from fish. A fish's tongue is pretty basic, just a fleshy fold that does not move very much. Land animals, on the other hand, need well-developed tongues to aid in masticating (breaking apart) their food and catching prey. The frog has a splendid example of a long, strong, flexible tongue.

When it is at rest, a frog's tongue is folded back on the floor of the mouth, with the tip pointed towards the throat. Here it lies ready to snap out at some unsuspecting insect, the way you might pick up and crack a neatly coiled whip. The frog's tongue is protrusible, which means that strong muscles at its base allow it to move quickly and to extend far out of the mouth. Thick mucous on the tongue helps trap the insects so they can be brought back into the mouth.

Magnified, a frog's taste buds look like tiny cauliflowers. They are similar to yours and are located just under the surface of the tongue. When the frog flips its tongue out of its mouth, the taste buds are spread out over the entire tip. This means that the frog can actually taste better when its tongue is out of the mouth than when it is neatly folded up inside.

Painted reed frog

AMPHIBIAN MENU

What do amphibians like to eat? Salamanders eat mostly insects, spiders, and sow bugs. Some tadpoles are vegetarians, but most tend to feed on whatever food is available in their environment, mostly microscopic protozoans and bacteria. Frogs are carnivorous, which means they eat flesh. They are content to eat worms, insects, other amphibians, and even small mammals. The marine toad has been known to snack on dog food if it is available.

The frog's sticky tongue is long, flexible, and swift. At rest it is folded back on the bottom of the mouth, with the tip pointed towards the throat. It flies forward and out of the mouth to snap up insects.

Argentine horned frog, facing page

HummingBirds

(Family: Trochilidae)

These tiny birds whir through the air like flying jewels, buzzing from flower to flower and hovering in midair to drink nectar. Hummingbirds need a lot of energy to keep themselves aloft, so it's no wonder they eat almost constantly. A single hummingbird requires nectar from more than a thousand flower blossoms each day to satisfy its hunger. As a rule, hummingbirds eat mostly floral nectar and small insects.

Originally, scientists thought the tongue of the hummingbird was hollow and could suck up flower nectar the way you might sip juice through a straw. But the hummingbird's tongue actually forks in two. Each half is made of tough membrane that curls up into a feeding trough. Tiny tubes on the tongue pull the flower nectar into the tongue troughs. If small insects are caught by the tongue, the hummingbird eats them as well.

If you could get a hummingbird to stick out its tongue at you, you might notice another interesting feature. The membrane of the tongue is sometimes fringed. This is from all the wear and tear the tongue goes through as it gathers nectar and catches insects. Although a hummer is unlikely to stick its tongue out at you, it has no trouble doing so. The tongue is protrusible, like the frog's, which means that a special mechanism of fine muscles rolls it in and out of the mouth.

The hummingbird loves sugar, which is the taste it detects best. Experiments with dishes of different solutions set out to attract the bright hummers show that these birds definitely prefer the sweeter solutions. They also like a thicker solution. In fact, hummingbirds are attracted to anything that resembles flower nectar.

Rufous hummingbird

SWALLOW IT WHOLE

Certain tropical fruit-eating birds, such as tanagers, are very sensitive to sugar. Tanagers have particularly keen taste organs because of the way they take their food. They crush fruit with their bills, releasing a stream of juice right onto their tongues. Birds that swallow their fruit whole are less sensitive to taste. Try gulping a small piece of a cherry or grape right down your throat. Can you taste it?

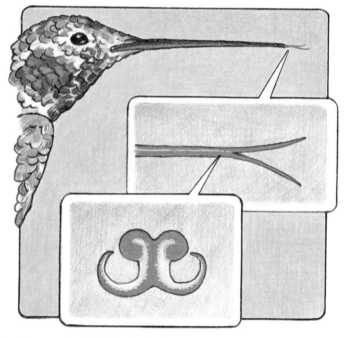

The hummingbird's forked tongue forms a double trough through which the bird sucks up nectar.

Ruby-throated hummingbird, facing page

Catfish

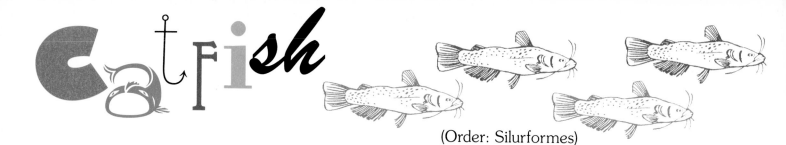

(Order: Silurformes)

If you eat a potato chip, you know it's salty as soon as you put it in your mouth. But a catfish can sense a salty food even from a distance. How? It has taste-sensitive cells (chemoreceptors) all over its body. They help the catfish recognize different tastes and even give clues about how far away the food source is. These fish spend their lives in the murky waters of lakes, rivers, and seas. Underwater, it is too dark to see well, and these creatures have poor vision. Taste is the catfish's most important sense.

Each catfish has several hundred thousand chemoreceptors on its body. The mouth and gill area alone boasts more than 20,000. Another 20,000 are concentrated on the fish's barbels ("whiskers") and fins. These chemoreceptors are like tiny detectors, always on the alert.

Magnified, they look somewhat like wide bottles, and they stick together like the sections of an orange. They are usually located underneath a tiny opening in the skin or mucous membrane.

How does the catfish's sense of taste (and smell, which is related) help it judge the distance of a food source? When the first taste of a food chemical is detected, the catfish spreads its barbels. Then it moves its head slowly from side to side and starts to swim toward the food source. The fish compares the concentrations of taste on the different parts of its body to determine how far away it is from a possible meal. As the scent and taste grow stronger, the fish swims faster. Then it zeros in on its dinner, mostly smaller fish.

Tiger shovelnose catfish

TASTE TEST

Fish respond to the same basic taste groups that humans respond to: bitter, sweet, salty, and sour. A bitter taste is often determined by the presence of quinine or other alkaloids. Sweetness is detectable by the presence of sugar. A substance that tastes salty will have—you guessed it—salt in it. (Another word for salt is sodium.) Certain acids are used to check for a sour taste.

Taste-sensitive cells dot the catfish's body and are very numerous around the mouth. In reality, these cells are invisible.

Siluris glanis, facing page

Lizards

(Order: Sauria)

The lizard's flicking, forked tongue is a well-known characteristic of this animal, but what purpose does it serve? As a rule, lizards have hard, scaly snouts, and their lips do not move. So their tongues have to do a lot of work to gather food. In crocodiles and most turtles the tongue simply lies on the bottom of the mouth. But the lizard's tongue is very flexible. In some lizards, the tongue even has scaly pads as protection from the animal's own sharp lower teeth. In most lizards the tongue is forked. The monitor lizard's tongue is so deeply forked it resembles the snake's.

Lizards flick their tongues in and out of their mouths to investigate their surroundings and to locate their food. When the tips of the tongue are out of the mouth, they "catch" tiny chemical particles in the air. When the tongue is withdrawn into the mouth, it feeds these particles into two pits on the roof of the lizard's mouth. These pits are called Jacobson's organs, and they process both odors and tastes. Chemoreceptors within the organs send signals to the lizard's brain, which then determines what action the animal should take in response to the chemical. If the brain interprets the odor or taste as food, the lizard will hunt its prey down (usually ants). If it detects a viper, a type of snake that feeds on lizards, the animal will take evasive action. Interestingly, the lizard's tongue-darting is influenced by temperature. The warmer it is, the more the lizard will flick its tongue.

Basilisk lizard

TONGUE TYPES

Rainbow lizards have short fleshy tongues, unlike monitor lizards. Rainbows do not use their tongues to search for food, because their tongues are less sensitive. Rather, this lizard sights its prey with its eyes. The gecko's tongue is similar to the rainbow lizard's, but it is rounded at the front and the tip is just notched, rather than fully forked. Taste buds are located on the undersides of these lizards' tongues.

The Komodo dragon, like many lizards, flicks its forked tongue in and out of its mouth to bring taste molecules to the sense organ on the roof of its mouth.

Collared lizard, facing page

SHEEP

(Genus: *Ovis*)

Sheep

Lambs just one week old begin to learn to eat the foods adult sheep eat, in addition to their mother's milk. The sheep's food preferences are partly innate (inborn) and partly learned. Like humans, sheep have taste buds on their tongues. These respond to the four basic tastes of bitter, sweet, salty, and sour. Some of the sheep's taste buds are most responsive to salty and sour tastes. Others are tuned to sweet, quinine (bitter), and acidic tastes.

Have you ever tasted a drop of your blood? It's salty, isn't it? Well, sheep's saliva is even saltier than blood, about five times saltier. And the animal produces plenty of it—up to 30 pints (about 15 liters) a day! Salty saliva is an important part of this animal's digestive system. Here's why.

Sheep are ruminants, along with goats, cattle, deer, and buffalo. Ruminants are mammals with cloven hooves that chew cud. Cud is food that is partially digested in the animal's first stomach (called the rumen) and then returned to the mouth for another go-around. The saliva in the mouth contains a substance called an alkali, which neutralizes the digestive acid from the animal's rumen. Alkalis form salt, which is why the sheep's saliva is so high in sodium (salt). The sheep's need for salt explains why this animal, and other ruminants, are so fond of salt licks.

DIFFERENT TASTES

Calves are much more sensitive to sucrose (table sugar) than humans are, but they don't care much for saccharin, an artificial sweetener. The laboratory rat likes sucrose and saccharin, but the cat is indifferent to both. All species (and individuals of a single species) have different taste preferences and sensitivities. That's good from an ecological point of view. Imagine how much competition for certain foods there would be if all animals preferred the same tastes. Diversity in taste perception helps make sure there is enough to go around.

Like humans, sheep have taste buds on their tongues. Their digestive system depends heavily on salt.

Bighorn ram, facing page

WOODPECKers

(Family: Picidae)

Pileated woodpecker

If you have ever been awakened by what sounded like an electric drill but was only a bird, you know just how much noise a woodpecker can make! The woodpecker uses its hard beak to drill, hammer, and crack open tree bark in search of insects and larvae. This bird can even split open a nut for the meat inside.

The woodpecker's beak may be a power tool, but its tongue is a delicate instrument. It is slender and, in some woodpeckers, ends in a barbed tip useful for spearing insects. The green woodpecker has a long snaky tongue, thickly coated with saliva, which is perfect for probing ant nests. The sticky coating traps the insects so they can be pulled back into the woodpecker's mouth. The woodpecker's saliva serves another purpose as well. When ants are disturbed, they secrete a bitter acid. The woodpecker's saliva, like the sheep's, contains an alkali that neutralizes the acid, making it possible for the bird to eat the bitter insects.

How does the woodpecker's long tongue fit in its small head? Actually, the tongue only looks impressively long. It is attached to delicate bones and a very elastic tissue. This apparatus is known as the hyoid. When the hyoid slides upward in the woodpecker's neck, the tongue can stick out, sometimes as far as four inches. The hyoid gives the tongue its flexibility and reach.

TWIG TOOL

When the famous naturalist Charles Darwin was on the Galapagos Islands, he discovered an interesting woodpecker finch. This bird likes to eat the grubs that bore into the bark of trees, but does not have a long enough bill to reach them. Instead, the woodpecker finch picks up a twig or a cactus needle and pokes it into the grub's hole, neatly skewering its meal. Scientists believe that this is the only bird that uses tools.

The woodpecker's tongue is attached to delicate bones and elastic tissue that curve around the bird's skull and, in some cases, enter the right nostril.

Greater spotted woodpecker, facing page

CHameleons

(Family: Chamaeleonidae)

Old World chameleon

What can you do in $\frac{1}{25}$ of a second? Not much, but a chameleon can zap an insect in that tiny fraction of time. How? With its long, sticky tongue, which can reach a distance greater than the chameleon's body and tail combined. Like most reptiles, the chameleon is a stalker. It first climbs to a place where it can scan for insects. After it spots its prey, it slowly creeps forward. When it is within reach of the hapless insect, the chameleon extends its tongue with lightning speed and snatches its prey.

The chameleon's tongue is amazingly long when extended and ends in a swollen club shape. Mucous glands secrete a sticky coating on this tip to trap insects. When a chameleon prepares to strike, it first aims its head at the insect. Then it draws its tongue to the front of its jaws. Finally, a special accelerator muscle shoots the tongue tip off its slippery resting place and out of the mouth.

Besides being sticky, the tongue tip is very strong. It may even help the chameleon grasp larger prey, just as the tip of an elephant's trunk grasps pieces of food. Bigger chameleon species capture locusts and other insects that are probably too powerful to be trapped by adhesive action alone. What does the animal do with its extra-long tongue when it's not zapping its dinner? It scrunches it up inside its mouth, like a sweater pushed up at the sleeve.

CHAMELEON HABITS AND HABITATS

Chameleons are usually arboreal (tree-dwelling), but some live on land. Most of the 80 species are found in Africa, yet these quick-change artists can also be found in Asia as far east as India. Madagascar is famous for its variety of chameleons. Chameleons turn their brightest colors when they are annoyed, and females sport vibrant hues just before they lay their eggs.

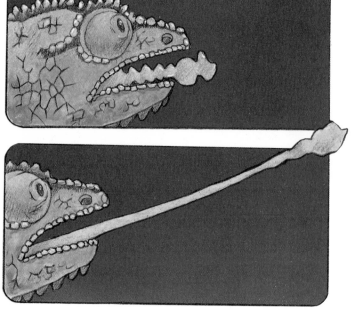

When the chameleon's long tongue is inside the mouth, it is bunched up like a sweater pushed up at the sleeve. When it is fully extended to catch an insect, the tongue can reach farther than the animal's body and tail combined.

Flap-necked chameleon, facing page

190

DEER

(Family: Cervidae)

Have you ever seen a deer in a forest? It sniffs around and eats certain leaves or twigs. It seems to find some more appealing than others. This is called browsing, and it is similar to a shopper trying on different clothes before making a purchase. What the deer finally selects is most likely to meet its nutritional needs.

Deer are herbivores, which means they eat plants. They may eat grasses, sedges, nuts, fruits, and mushrooms, as well as the bark of trees or shrubs. They're also drawn to salt licks, especially when salt is missing from their diet.

How are deer able to select the food that's right for them? Their sense of taste serves them well. Chemoreceptors in their nose and on their tongue respond to the chemicals in air, water, and substances. These chemoreceptors also help deer avoid many poisons. Black-tailed deer, for example, refuse even a nibble of a certain ragwort that is poisonous.

Wild deer seem to need salt. Why? Maybe they just like the taste of it. In fact, some evidence shows that the taste for salt is acquired (learned), both in humans and in animals. Yet deer seem to crave salt depending on the chemical contents of the water and food available. Their salt hunger varies with the season. If deer require salt, it is usually in the spring, when animals forage for fresh green foods. They also crave salt for five or six weeks after fawning (giving birth). Salt licks may also provide trace elements and minerals necessary for the deer's nutrition.

Does your grandmother make a special dessert that's delicious? Just as human cultures have food preferences passed on from generation to generation, the doe's choice of food influences her fawns. For deer, food selection may be learned.

Mule deer

SALT CRAVING

Wild deer near Jackson Hole, Wyoming, travel for miles to reach the nearest salt lick. They have worn great trails over many years to get to the salt. They eat the earth at the lick for the salt or alkali it contains. Without it, the deer become sluggish and lose energy.

Deer browse on trees and shrubs. They taste with chemoreceptors in their nose and on their tongue.

White-tailed deer, facing page

Octopuses

(Family: Octopodidae)

Sitting silently near its rocky lair an octopus awaits dinner. The eight-legged animal camouflages itself and blends with the murky ocean floor. An unsuspecting crab creeps by. Slowly, the octopus unrolls one tentacle and gently fondles the passing creature. Satisfied that it has found food, the octopus draws the crab towards its beak-like mouth and begins to eat.

How did the octopus identify the crab? It can taste by touch. The animal's body is riddled with nerve endings that sense changes in the environment. The suckers on the octopus' tentacles contain the greatest number of these nerve endings. In fact, a single sucker carries tens of thousands of such cells. In all, the octopus' body contains about 3 billion nerve endings!

Most of these nerve endings, or receptors, sense chemicals and so are called chemoreceptors. They are similar to human taste buds and allow the octopus to taste each object it touches. Indeed, octopuses can distinguish objects by taste as well as they can with their keen eyesight. Perhaps it is more accurate to think of the octopus' tentacles as eight rubbery, dangling tongues, which lick and probe the sea bottom in search of the next meal.

Generally, octopuses do not venture far from their rocky lairs. Their ability to taste by touch allows these shy creatures to detect food nearby. When food particles pass near the surface of the animal's tentacle, the suckers expand and reach out in the direction of the food source. The octopus can then seize its prey without ever having to leave the security of its neighborhood. Octopuses can taste sweet, sour, and bitter solutions ten to a thousand times better than humans can. They can even taste whether the surrounding water is more or less salty than usual.

Lesser octopus

STINKY INK

Octopuses eject an inky secretion when pursued by a predator. This was once considered a "smoke-screen" that enabled the creature to make a quick getaway. However, most animals that hunt the octopus have poor eyesight and instead rely on their keen sense of smell to locate their victim. The inky cloud actually dulls the olfactory (smell) nerves of the predator, allowing the octopus to escape.

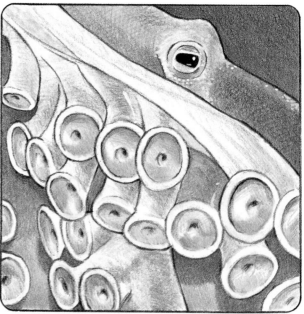

The octopus tastes by touch with the suckers on its eight tentacles.

Octopus briareus, facing page

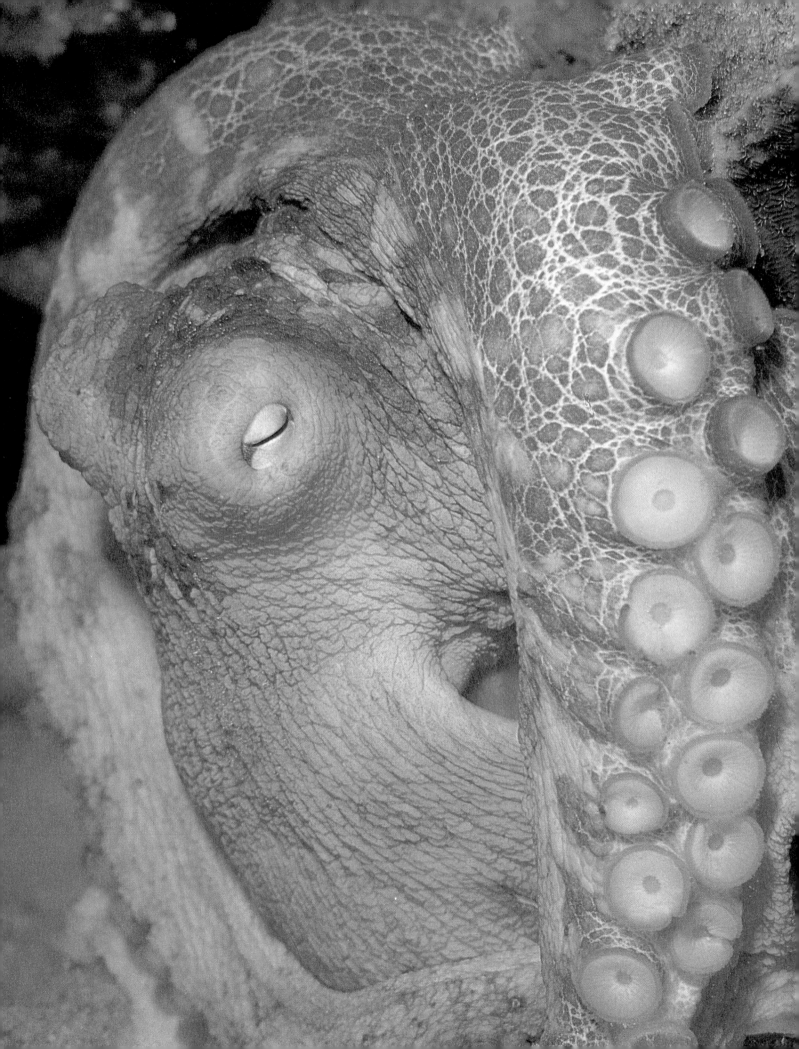

Snakes

(Order: Squamata)

Like lizards, snakes sport forked tongues that dart in and out of their mouths. Yet this slithering creature's tongue is one of the few in the world with zero taste buds. The snake cannot taste at all with its tongue. Nevertheless, the tongue is very important to the snake's survival.

For starters, snakes use their tongues to scare away predators. When alarmed, a snake draws back its head, hisses violently, and flickers its tongue wildly. The darting tongue adds to the animal's threatening appearance and serves to warn enemies that the snake is ready to strike. The snake's tongue is also crucial to its success as a hunter. The tongues of certain creatures, such as the frog and the chameleon, snatch insects up and draw them into the mouth. Instead of insects, the snake's tongue "catches" invisible tastes and odor particles in the air. These chemical particles are then carried back into the mouth where, with each point of the forked tongue, they are fed into two pits on the roof of the snake's mouth. These pits are called Jacobson's organs. Receptor cells in these organs send a signal to the reptile's brain. If the brain interprets the signal as a tasty meal, you can be sure the snake will follow its tongue and hungrily hunt its prey.

FUNKY FOLKLORE

The function of the snake's fantastic tongue remained a mystery for centuries. Some fanciful theories were that the tongue served to lap up liquids, to keep the snake's nose clean, to lick prey before swallowing, to serve as a feeler, or to function as a stinger. The ancient Greeks believed that prophets could tell the future by having their ears cleaned by the tongues of serpents. The Greek philosopher Aristotle (384-322 B.C.) believed that the two tips of the snake's tongue gave the animal double pleasure when it tasted.

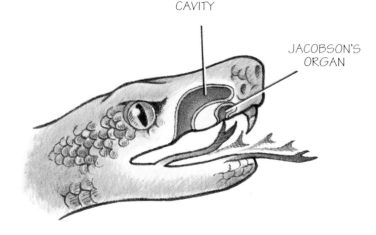

The snake uses its tongue to carry taste and odor molecules into the special sensor in its mouth, called the Jacobson's organ.

Broad-banded copperhead, facing page

ANTeaters

(Family: Tachyglossidae)

Giant anteater

Even though it's called an anteater, this odd-looking mammal eats ants, termites, or even worms, depending on what's available. And how does it catch these creatures? With its sticky, speedy tongue. The anteater can extrude (stick out) its long tongue about 100 times per minute!

Not only is the anteater's tongue super-fast, it is covered with a sticky secretion. This thick, transparent liquid is produced by the animal's large salivary glands. If you were to touch just one drop and then let go, the secretion would stick to you. You could stretch it into thin strands up to a foot (30 centimeters) long, just as if it were taffy. This secretion acts as a glue to trap the insects on the anteater's tongue. Stuck to the tongue, they are drawn back into the animal's mouth.

Then what happens? The anteater doesn't have any teeth, and it's difficult to swallow that many ants whole. So the tongue performs yet another task: it masticates the food, which means that it breaks it into pulp, as you do when you chew. Blood rushes into the tongue, making it very stiff and larger than usual. In this state, the tongue is strong enough even to break open termite tunnels in wood. But the tongue becomes mightier still. Barbed, teethlike spines rise up on the top of the anteater's tongue. These grind against the spines on the roof of the anteater's mouth and smash the insects to pieces.

WHAT'S IN A NAME?

There are several different species of anteaters. The great anteater can reach a length of six feet and is sometimes called an ant bear. Silky anteaters have soft fur and short snouts. Spiny anteaters have quills like porcupines and curl themselves into a poky ball when threatened. Another name for an anteater is echidna. The animal's scientific family name, tachyglossidae, means "fast tongue."

The anteater probes a log with its long, sticky tongue, searching for ants or termites.

Tamandua tetradactyla, *facing page*

DOLPHins

(Family: Delphinidae)

The dolphin's natural grace and interesting behavior have awed people for ages. These highly intelligent, friendly marine mammals recognize each other, travel in schools, and have specific preferences for certain fish. The animals' complex actions baffled scientists for years.

It has since been discovered that dolphins have an excellent sense of taste that governs much of their behavior. Dolphins have numerous fleshy grooves and ridges on the base of their tongues called papillae (rhymes with happily). The papillae house many taste buds, which are similar to those found in humans and herbivorous (plant-eating) animals. These taste buds are remarkably sensitive and can detect traces of chemicals that have been dissolved in the ocean water. In favorable currents, these dissolved chemicals are carried over great distances.

Dolphins periodically open their mouths as they swim in order to taste these waterborne chemicals. Fish leave behind a chemical trail, like Hansel and Gretel's bread crumbs. By following the taste of this trail a dolphin can accurately locate its prey. Dolphins are also able to swim in schools by following the tastes of their schoolmates.

Dolphins, like humans, can taste sweet, sour, salty, and bitter substances. However, unlike humans, they do not seem to mind a bitter flavor. Dolphins in captivity are known to show definite preferences for certain fish. In fact, dolphins learn more quickly when they are given a favorite fish as a reward—perhaps it's like receiving ice cream instead of spinach after doing a good deed!

FACT OR FICTION?

Mythology is full of stories involving dolphins. In ancient times, dolphins were said to be gifted with human intelligence. Some tales told of a dolphin befriending a favored child, who could take rides on the dolphin's back. Other legends celebrated dolphins that saved shipwrecked victims from certain death by carrying them to shore. In one myth, the son of the heroic wanderer Odysseus fell into the sea and was saved by a dolphin. Odysseus honored the dolphin by engraving its image on a ring he wore always.

Dolphins open their mouths from time to time as they swim to taste the chemicals in the water. These chemicals help the animals locate prey and follow the trails of the other dolphins in their school.

Bottle-nosed dolphin, above and facing page

INDEX

This glossarized index will help you find specific information about the senses of hearing, sight, touch, smell, and taste or explain the meanings of some of the words used throughout this book.

acoustic—related to sound or to the sense of hearing

acoustics—the scientific study of how sound is produced, transported, and received

acuity, see visual acuity

agility—the ability to move quickly and easily

amphibian—animal that can live both on land and in water, 134, 152, 178

anteaters, 198

antenna—one of a pair of thin, sensitive projections on the heads of many insects and some crustaceans that carry the organs for hearing, touch, and smell, 85, 86, 90, 94, 124, 126, 130, 166, 170, 172, 174

antennae—plural of antenna

ants, 128

astigmatism—visual defect caused by an uneven cornea, which prevents focusing on sharp, distinct images, 68

audible—able to be heard

auditory—related to the sense of hearing, from Latin "to hear"

auditory canal—the tube through which sound waves travel from the outer ear to the middle and inner ear, 7, 36, 42

balance—the state of being stable and steady; also called equilibrium, 7, 14

barbel—whisker-like organ of touch, taste, and smell made of bone and cartilage; the catfish has three or four pairs of barbels, 85, 182

bats, 8, 22, 138

bees, 130, 166

beetles, 52

bifocal—two-lensed, 56

binocular vision—type of vision in which both eyes move and work together to see a single image, 45, 66, 72, 80, 82

bioacoustics—the scientific study of the sounds made by living things; "bio" means "life," 12

birds, 26, 142, 156

blowflies, 168

butterflies, 94, 172

camouflage—concealing oneself by taking cover in the natural environment or by changing color, 54, 64, 66, 70

catfish, 182

cats, 76, 108, 146

centimeter—unit of measurement in metric system, equal to 0.4 inches

chameleons, 54, 66, 190

chemoreceptor—cell that receives chemical particles that give substances their taste and smell; chemoreceptors convert this sensation into an electrical impulse and send it to the brain, 163, 164, 168, 170, 172, 174, 182, 192

cockroaches, 170

compound eyes—type of eye that insects and many crustaceans have, made up of hundreds of tiny lenses, adapted to perceive slight movement rather than distinct shapes, 45, 50, 52, 58, 60

cones—photosensitive cells in the retina that detect colors in bright light, 44, 166

cornea—membrane through which light passes into the eye, covers the lens, 44, 74, 76

crabs, 60, 70, 98, 174

crickets, 10

crocodiles, 112, 184

crustacean—aquatic animal with a segmented body and a hard shell, such as the lobster, crab, and shrimp, 174,

Darwin, Charles—a famous British naturalist (1809–1882); developed the theory of evolution, 164, 188

decibel—the unit used to measure the intensity (volume) of sound, 6, 34

deer, 192

depth perception—ability to judge distance, 45, 64, 26, 70

dogs, 28, 68, 154

dolphins, 30, 200

domesticated—tamed; in the service of humans, such as cattle and sheep

dormant—in a state of rest or inactivity, 92

dragonflies, 58

drumfish, 12

duck, 102

eardrum—membrane that acts like a drum to collect sound waves and pass them on to the middle ear; also called tympanic membrane, 7, 8, 10, 14, 26, 36

earthworms, 164

echolocation—the ability of an animal, such as a bat or a dolphin, to orient itself by producing noise and listening for the returning echo, 22, 24, 30, 32, 36, 42

electromagnetic spectrum—the full range of light frequencies scientists have detected with equipment; the visible spectrum, the range of colors humans can see with the naked eye, is only a tiny slice of the full range, which includes infrared and ultraviolet light, 44

elephants, 38, 80, 160

endangered—faced with the threat of extinction, or dying out, 104, 112, 132, 160

equilibrium—balance, 7, 14

family—third-narrowest category of taxonomy

far-sighted, able to see distant objects better than near ones, 72

feelers—organs that detect tactile sensation; in insects and some crustaceans, these are antennae, 85

fiddler crabs, 98

field of vision, see visual field

fish, 12, 56, 176, 182

fly, 168

forage—to search for and gather food

four-eyed fish, 56

foxes, 20

frequency—the number of times a sound wave vibrates per second; measured in hertz, 6, 18, 22, 28, 30, 32, 34, 38, 40, 42

frogs, 14, 64, 132, 134, 178

fruit-eating bats, 138

geckos, 116

genera—plural of genus

genus—second-narrowest category of taxonomy

gerbils, 136

grasshoppers, 10, 90

gustation—the act of tasting or the sense of taste, from the Latin gustare, "to taste", 162

habitat—an animal's natural environment; living space, 20, 24, 106, 152

hawks, 78

hertz—the unit used to measure frequency; 1 hertz equals 1 sound wave cycle per second, 6, 28

hummingbird, 180

hyoid—mechanism of bone and tissue that extends and retracts the tongue, 188

iguanas, green, 100

inaudible—unable to be heard

infrared—very low-frequency light invisible to human eye, produces heat, 44, 52, 62

infrasound—very low-frequency sound inaudible to the human ear, 38, 42

inner ear, 7, 12, 14, 16, 26, 30, 40, 42

insects, 86, 90, 94, 166, 168, 170, 172

intensity—the volume of a sound, how loud or soft it is; measured in decibels, 6, 34

invertebrate—an animal without a backbone, such as mollusks and crustaceans, 50, 70

iris—colored part of the eye that expands and contracts the pupil, 44, 64, 74

Jacobson's organ—sense organ on the roof of reptiles' mouths that detects smell and taste, 140, 146, 184, 196

Johnston's organ—organ at the base of some insects' antennae that helps the animal maintain its balance and orientation, 94

kangaroo rats, 18

kilogram—unit of measurement in metric system, equal to 2.2 pounds

kiwis, 142

labellum—spongy pad at the base of a blowfly's proboscis, which the insect uses to probe substances; the hairs on the labellum detect sucrose, 168

labyrinth—another word for the inner ear, so-called because it resembles a maze of interconnecting passages, 12, 14

lemurs, 150

lens—part of eye that focuses light on the retina, 44, 76

lizards, 184

lobster, 174

mallards, 102

masticate—break up food in the mouth; chew, 178, 198

metamorphosis—a change in form between immature and adult animals, mainly frogs and insects; for example, as they develop into frogs, water-dwelling tadpoles lose their tails and grow legs, and they become amphibious, able to live both in water and on land, 14, 134

meter—unit of measurement in metric system, equal to 3.3 feet

middle ear, 7, 12, 18, 26, 40

minnows, 176
moles, 110
monkeys, 34
monocular vision—type of vision in which the eyes move independently of the other, seeing separate images, 45, 54, 66, 80, 82
moray eels, 106
mosquitoes, 124
moths, 8, 126

nasal cavity—cavity inside the head in which olfactory receptors receive scent particles, 123, 132, 140
nasal passage—part of the nose leading from the nostrils to the nasal cavities, 123
near-sighted, able to see near objects better than distant ones, 74
nerve—a bundle of fiber that conveys impulses to the nervous system and the brain
nictitating membrane—membrane that covers and protects the eye from irritants and objects, 72
nocturnal—active at night; nocturnal animals generally hunt or forage at night and sleep during the day, 18, 32, 76, 116, 138, 142

octopuses, 70, 194
oilbirds, 32
olfaction—the sense of smell, 122
olfactory—related to the sense of smell, 122, 150, 170
olfactory lobe—the part of the brain that interprets smells, 123, 138, 146, 158
olfactory pits, 130, 148
olfactory receptor—a cell that receives smells, 123, 146, 148, 152, 154
optic nerve—nerve that carries visual impulses to brain, 44
orangutans, 120
orb web spiders, 88
order—fourth-largest category of taxonomy
owls, 40, 72

pain, 85
papillae—tiny bumps and grooves on the tongue that house taste buds, 200
penguins, 74
peripheral vision—what we see "out of the corner of our eye," side vision, 68, 72, 74

pheromone—a substance secreted by an animal that influences the behavior of other animals of the same species. Pheromones are perceived by the sense of smell, 122, 128, 130, 136, 146, 150, 170
photosensitive—sensitive to light, 44, 46, 60
pinna—the external part of the ear, also called outer ear, 6, 22
pinnae—plural of pinna, 22
pit organ—a cavity on the heads of some snakes that senses heat given off by warm-blooded prey; usually, pit organs are located under and in front of the snake's eyes, 62, 140
pitch—how high or low a sound is; determined by the frequency of the sound wave, 6, 26
platypuses, 114
prairie dogs, 144
praying mantis, 86
proboscis—the slender beak of some insects, used for sucking and piercing; the elephant's trunk is also called a proboscis, 80, 166, 168, 172
prostomium—an earthworm's primitive mouth, 164
protrusible—able to be thrust forward, as the tongue of the chameleon and hummingbird, 178, 180
pupil—round hole in the center of the iris, expands and contracts to admit or shut out light, 44, 62, 72, 76

reptile—a cold-blooded vertebrate that typically has scaly skin, such as the crocodile, the snake, and the scorpion, 92, 112, 132, 190
resolving power, see visual acuity
retina—light-sensitive membrane in inner eye that sends images to the brain via the optic nerve, 44, 52, 54, 56, 76
rods—photosensitive cells in the retina that detect dim light and record images in black and white, 44, 72
ruminant—a mammal with cloven hooves that chews cud; includes sheep, deer, cows, goats, and buffalo, 186

salamanders, 152
salmon, 148
salt, 186, 192
sand scorpions, 92
scallops, 48
sea horses, 54
seals, 36

semicircular canals— this organ signals the brain when it senses a loss of balance, 7

sensilla—plural of sensillum, a hair-like sense organ consisting of one cell or a few cells; mosquitoes and other insects have sensilla on their antennae, 85, 86, 90, 92, 94, 126, 130

sharks, 158

sheep, 186

shrews, 24

shrimp, 174

sloths, 104

snakes, 16, 62, 140, 196

sonar—stands for Sound Navigation Ranging, humans' electronic method of echolocation; this system uses sounds and their returning echoes to locate objects underwater, 30, 32

songbirds, 26

sound wave—the vibrations that produce sound; these move in waves through a medium such as air, earth, or water, 6

spawning—to deposit eggs; after salmon spawn, they die, 148

species—narrowest category of taxonomy; members of a species look similar and can reproduce with each other

spiders, 50, 88, 96

starfish, 46

substances; the hairs on the labellum detect sucrose, 168

sucrose—a type of sugar present in cane and beets and processed to make table sugar, 168

sugar, 162, 166, 168, 172, 176, 180

tactile—related to the sense of touch, 84, 98

tarsus (plural, tarsi)—the tip of an insect's foot, 168, 172

taxonomy—scientific system of classification for all living things; the seven taxonomic categories, from broadest to narrowest, are kindgom, phylum, class, order, family, genus, species

tears, 62

tiger swallowtails, 94

toads, 134

touch receptor—cell that receives physical cues such as pressure, pain, texture, or temperature, 85, 98, 100, 102, 108

trap-door spider, 96

turkey vultures, 156

turtles, 132

tympanic membrane—thin membrane that acts like a drum to collect sound and pass it to the middle ear; in humans, it is commonly called the eardrum, and it separates the middle ear from the outer ear, 7, 8, 14

ultrasound—very high-frequency sound inaudible to the human ear, 6, 8, 22, 24

ultraviolet—very high-frequency light invisible to the human eye, 44, 60, 74, 92

vertebrate—an animal with a backbone, such as mammals and reptiles, 74

vibration—quivering; all movement produces vibrations; this is what makes sound, 6, 16, 38, 88, 96, 98, 108, 110

vibrissae—whisker-like organs of touch in the walrus, cat, and other mammals, 85, 108, 110, 118

visible spectrum, see also electromagnetic spectrum–range of colors

visual acuity (also called resolving power)—sharpness of vision, ability to focus on distinct shapes, 44, 76

visual field (also called field of vision)—the area you can see without moving your head from side to side or tilting it up and down; the human visual field is from shoulder to shoulder and forehead to waist, 45, 80, 82

visual pigment— a substance in the eyes that makes seeing possible, 44

vomeronasal organ—smelling organ on the roof of the mouths of dogs and cats, similar to the Jacobson's organ, 146, 154

walruses, 118

wave, see sound wave

whales, 42

woodpeckers, 188

zebras, 82

PHOTO CREDITS

(listed alphabetically by photographer's name)

Animals Animals © Doug Allan/Oxford Scientific Films p. 75; Animals Animals © R. H. Armstrong p. 180; Animals Animals © Kathie Atkinson/Oxford Scientific Films p. 128; Animals Animals © M. Austerman p. 160; Animals Animals © Carson Baldwin, Jr. p. 83; Photo Researchers, Inc. © John J. Bangma p. 33; Animals Animals © Anthony Bannister pp. 20, 37; Animals Animals © G. I. Bernard p. 171; Animals Animals © G. I. Bernard/Oxford Scientific Films pp. 49, 70, 113, 169, 194; Animals Animals © Hans and Judy Beste p. 115; Animals Animals © Aldo Brando p. 104; Animals Animals © W. Gregory Brown pp. 13, 54, 106, 195; Animals Animals © Betty K. Bruce p. 27; Animals Animals © George K. Bryce p. 168; Animals Animals © M. A. Chappell pp. 19, 86; Animals Animals © John Chellman pp. 80, 109, 120, 146, 147, 198, 201; Animals Animals © Ken Cole p. 15; Animals Animals © Margot Conte p. 102; Animals Animals © J. A. L. Cooke p. 125; Animals Animals © J. A. L. Cooke/Oxford Scientific Films p. 89; Animals Animals © Terry Cooke p. 39; Animals Animals © Dagmar p. 18; Animals Animals © Stephen Dalton pp. 8, 9, 14, 40, 58, 72, 90, 91, 126, 127, 130, 172, 190; Animals Animals © Stephen Dalton/Oxford Scientific Films p. 189; Animals Animals © Bruce Davidson pp. 38, 67, 76, 81; Animals Animals © E. R. Degginger pp. 31, 41, 46, 50, 95, 97, 101, 117, 164, 174; Animals Animals © Michael Dick pp. 25, 34; Animals Animals © Don Enger p. 144; Animals Animals © Michael Fogden pp. 129, 139, 140; Animals Animals © Mickey Gibson p. 77; Animals Animals © Arthur Gloor pp. 92, 178; Animals Animals © Ana Laura Gonzalez p. 82; Animals Animals © Richard Goss/Partridge Productions p. 24; Photo Researchers, Inc./National Audubon Society © Donald S. Heintzelman p. 73; Animals Animals © Holt Studios Int. pp. 165, 167; Animals Animals © Johnny Johnson pp. 74, 149; Animals Animals © Scott Johnson p. 175; Photo Researchers, Inc. © Joyce Photographics p. 186; Animals Animals © Breck P. Kent pp. 52, 116, 199; Animals Animals © Richard Kolar pp. 137, 145; Animals Animals © G. L. Kooyman p. 36; Animals Animals © Gérard Lacz pp. 28, 30, 68, 154, 200; Animals Animals © Richard K. La Val p. 22; Animals Animals © Zig Leszczynski pp. 12, 17, 48, 55, 56, 57, 63, 65, 71, 87, 93, 98, 112, 118, 133, 134, 136, 153, 170, 179, 182, 185, 192, 196; Photo Researchers, Inc. © Zig Leszczynski p. 191; Animals Animals © Bates Littlehales pp. 35, 152; Animals Animals © C. C. Lockwood p. 158; Animals Animals © Robert A. Lubeck pp. 62, 131, 181; Animals Animals © Robert Maier pp. 59, 103, 148, 183; Animals Animals © Joe McDonald pp. 79, 99, 121, 132, 141, 157, 197; Photo Researchers, Inc. © Tom McHugh pp. 114, 142, 143; Animals Animals © Raymond A. Mendez pp. 69, 88; Animals Animals © Colin Milkins/Oxford Scientific Films p. 47; Animals Animals © Sean Morris p. 96; Animals Animals © Terry G. Murphy p. 161; Animals Animals © Patti Murray pp. 26, 100; Animals Animals © Alan G. Nelson p. 21; Animals Animals © Oxford Scientific Films pp. 23, 66, 138; Animals Animals © Robert Pearcy p. 155; Photo Researchers, Inc./National Audubon Society © Robert E. Pelham p. 51; Animals Animals © Mark Pidgeon/Oxford Scientific Films p. 151; Animals Animals © Michael Pitts/Oxford Scientific Films p. 107; Animals Animals © K. G. Preston-Mafham pp. 10, 11, 184; Animals Animals © Juan M. Renjifo p. 32; Animals Animals © L. L. T. Rhodes p. 43; Animals Animals © Frank Roberts p. 150; Animals Animals © J. H. Robinson pp. 16, 64, 166, 173; Animals Animals © Leonard Lee Rue III p. 111; Animals Animals © C. W. Schwartz pp.78, 156, 193; Animals Animals © Alastair Shay/Oxford Scientific Films pp. 45, 61, 135; Animals Animals © Frank Sladek p. 119; Animals Animals © Perry D. Slocum p. 188 Animals Animals © D. R. Specker p. 124; Photo Researchers, Inc. © Alvin E. Staffan p. 177; Animals Animals © Tony Tilford/Oxford Scientific Films p. 110; Animals Animals © Klaus Uhlenhut p. 60; Animals Animals © James D. Watt p. 42; Animals Animals © James Watt p. 159; Animals Animals © Bruce M. Wellman p. 94; Photo Researchers, Inc. © Jeanne White p. 108; Animals Animals © Fred Whitehead p. 176; Animals Animals © Jack Wilburn pp. 53, 187; Animals Animals © Barbara J. Wright p. 29; Photo Researchers, Inc. © Dr. Paul A. Zahl p. 105.